TEACHER'S PET PUBLICATIONS

PUZZLE PACK
for
Travels with Charley

based on the book by
John Steinbeck

Written by
William T. Collins

© 2005 Teacher's Pet Publications
All Rights Reserved

The materials in this packet are copyrighted
by Teacher's Pet Publications, Inc.

These pages may be duplicated by the purchaser
for use in the purchaser's own classroom.

Copying any of these materials and distributing them
for any other purpose is a violation of the copyright laws.

© 2005 Teacher's Pet Publications, Inc.
www.tpet.com

INTRODUCTION

If you already own the LitPlan for this title, this Puzzle Pack will refresh your Unit Resource Materials and Vocabulary Resource Materials sections plus give you additional materials you can substitute into the tests. If you do not already have a complete LitPlan, these pages will give you some supplemental materials to use with your own plan. There are two main groups of materials: one set for unit words (such as characters' names, symbols, places, etc.) and one set for vocabulary words associated with the book.

WORD LIST

There is a word list for both the unit words and the vocabulary words. These lists show you which words are being used in the materials and the clues or definitions being used for those words. You may want to give students a word list with clues/definitions to help them, or you may want students to only have a word list (without clues/definitions) if you want them to work a little harder. Both are available for duplication. The word lists can also be your "calling key" for the bingo games.

FILL IN THE BLANK AND MATCHING

There are 4 each of the fill in the blank and matching worksheets for both the unit and vocabulary words. These pages can be used either as extra worksheets for students or as objective parts of a unit test. They can be done individually if students need extra help or as a whole class activity to review the material covered.

MAGIC SQUARES

The magic squares not only reinforce the material covered but also work on reasoning and math skills. Many teachers have told us that their students really enjoy doing these!

WORD SEARCH PUZZLES

The word search words go in all directions, as indicated on your answer keys. Two of the word search puzzles have the clues listed rather than the words. This makes the puzzle a little more difficult, but it reinforces the material better. Two word search puzzles have words only for students who find the clue puzzles too difficult.

CROSSWORD PUZZLES

Both unit and vocabulary word sections have 4 crossword puzzles.

BINGO CARDS

There are 32 individual bingo cards for the unit words and 32 individual bingo cards for the vocabulary words. You can use your word list as a "call list," calling the words at random and marking them off of your list as you go, or you could use the flash cards by cutting them apart and drawing the words at random from a hat (or box or whatever). To make a better review, you might ask for the definition and spelling of each word as you call it out–or you could call out the definitions and have students tell you the words they need to look for on the puzzle.

JUGGLE LETTERS

The vocabulary juggle letter game is intended to help students learn the spellings of the words. One sheet has the definitions listed on it as an extra help for students who need it or to reinforce the definitions if you choose to do so.

FLASH CARDS

We've included a set of vocabulary flash cards you can duplicate, cut, and fold for your students. Some teachers make a few sets for general use by the class; others make a set for each student. Some teachers duplicate them for each student and have the students cut & fold their own. You can cut out just the words and put them in a hat, have each student pick out one word and write the definition and a sentence for that word. Students then swap words and papers, with the next student adding a sentence of his own under the last one. You can have students swap as many times as you like. Each time the student will read the sentences written prior to his own and then add a sentence. You can cut out the words and definitions separately and play "I Have; Who Has?" Each student in the room draws a word and definition. The first student says, "I have (the name of the word). Who has the definition?" The student with the definition reads it then says, "I have (the name of the vocabulary word she has). Who has the definition?" The round continues until all words and definitions have been given.

Travels With Charley Word List

No.	Word	Clue/Definition
1.	ALLERGIC	Charley was ___ to insecticides
2.	AMBASSADOR	Hotel in Chicago: ___ East
3.	AVALON	Deer Isle was like ___
4.	BEARS	Charley wanted to fight them at Yellowstone
5.	CANADA	This country wouldn't let Charley in
6.	CANUCKS	Maine's migrant farmers
7.	CHARLEY	The poodle; companion to Mr. Steinbeck
8.	CHEERLEADERS	Group of white women gathered at school to protest desegregation
9.	CHICAGO	Place where Mr. Steinbeck's wife met him to visit
10.	CHILD	The Bad Lands seemed like the work of an evil ___
11.	COFFEE	It is the great get-together symbol
12.	COYOTES	Two cans of dog food were left for them
13.	DELLS	Wisconsin ___; formed by ice during the Ice Age
14.	ELEYNE	Fair ___; the boat
15.	FARGO	The east-west middle of the country was in ___, ND
16.	FIRE	Kind of sermon in Vermont: ___ & Brimstone
17.	GLACIERS	Responsible for wiping out most of the redwood trees
18.	HARBOR	Sag ___; starting point of the trip
19.	HARRY	Lonesome ___; previous occupant of the hotel room
20.	ICEBREAKER	Mr. Steinbeck used Charley as this with strangers
21.	MAINE	White Mountains are in this state
22.	MIND	Texas is a state of ___, according to Mr. Steinbeck
23.	MISSOURI	This river, according to Mr. Steinbeck, should have been the east-west middle of the country
24.	MOBILE	These homes were revolutionary
25.	MOJAVE	Desert Mr. Steinbeck and Charley crossed
26.	MONTANA	State Mr. Steinbeck considered a great splash of grandeur
27.	ORLEANS	New ___; place where the Cheerleaders demonstrated
28.	POLITICS	Topic of family arguments
29.	POTATO	Mr. Steinbeck wanted to see these crops in Maine
30.	QUIXOTE	Rocinante was named for Don ___'s horse
31.	RABIES	Charley didn't have his certificate of vaccination for this
32.	REDWOOD	These trees cause wonder & respect in man
33.	ROBBIE	He wanted to be a hairdresser
34.	ROCINANTE	The truck
35.	SALINAS	Mr. Steinbeck's home town in California
36.	STEINBECK	Author
37.	TEXAS	Only state to enter the union by treaty
38.	THOUGHT	A man has to have feelings and then words before he can come close to this
39.	TRAVELS	___ With Charley
40.	TRIP	You don't take one, one takes you
41.	TRUCKERS	They have their own language, according to Mr. Steinbeck
42.	TRUTH	Near the end of the book, Mr. Steinbeck gave reasons why he couldn't find the ___ about the country
43.	TWIN	Minneapolis & St. Paul are the ___ Cities
44.	VACILANDO	Going somewhere with a direction in mind but not caring if you get there or not
45.	VIRGINIA	In this state Mr. Steinbeck realized his trip had ended
46.	WIFE	The boat was named for Steinbeck's

Travels With Charley Fill In The Blanks 1

1. Rocinante was named for Don ___'s horse
2. Maine's migrant farmers
3. Sag ___; starting point of the trip
4. The boat was named for Steinbeck's
5. Two cans of dog food were left for them
6. Going somewhere with a direction in mind but not caring if you get there or not
7. It is the great get-together symbol
8. Charley was ___ to insecticides
9. The Bad Lands seemed like the work of an evil ____
10. The truck
11. These trees cause wonder & respect in man
12. Group of white women gathered at school to protest desegregation
13. ____ With Charley
14. Deer Isle was like ____
15. Topic of family arguments
16. Mr. Steinbeck's home town in California
17. A man has to have feelings and then words before he can come close to this
18. He wanted to be a hairdresser
19. White Mountains are in this state
20. Mr. Steinbeck wanted to see these crops in Maine

Travels With Charley Fill In The Blanks 1 Answer Key

QUIXOTE	1. Rocinante was named for Don ___'s horse
CANUCKS	2. Maine's migrant farmers
HARBOR	3. Sag ___; starting point of the trip
WIFE	4. The boat was named for Steinbeck's
COYOTES	5. Two cans of dog food were left for them
VACILANDO	6. Going somewhere with a direction in mind but not caring if you get there or not
COFFEE	7. It is the great get-together symbol
ALLERGIC	8. Charley was ___ to insecticides
CHILD	9. The Bad Lands seemed like the work of an evil ___
ROCINANTE	10. The truck
REDWOOD	11. These trees cause wonder & respect in man
CHEERLEADERS	12. Group of white women gathered at school to protest desegregation
TRAVELS	13. ___ With Charley
AVALON	14. Deer Isle was like ___
POLITICS	15. Topic of family arguments
SALINAS	16. Mr. Steinbeck's home town in California
THOUGHT	17. A man has to have feelings and then words before he can come close to this
ROBBIE	18. He wanted to be a hairdresser
MAINE	19. White Mountains are in this state
POTATO	20. Mr. Steinbeck wanted to see these crops in Maine

Travels With Charley Fill In The Blanks 2

1. Rocinante was named for Don ___'s horse
2. Texas is a state of ____, according to Mr. Steinbeck
3. These homes were revolutionary
4. Mr. Steinbeck's home town in California
5. Fair ___; the boat
6. The Bad Lands seemed like the work of an evil ____
7. Charley didn't have his certificate of vaccination for this
8. Responsible for wiping out most of the redwood trees
9. ____ With Charley
10. Place where Mr. Steinbeck's wife met him to visit
11. Sag ___; starting point of the trip
12. New ___; place where the Cheerleaders demonstrated
13. The boat was named for Steinbeck's
14. Charley was ___ to insecticides
15. Maine's migrant farmers
16. You don't take one, one takes you
17. These trees cause wonder & respect in man
18. He wanted to be a hairdresser
19. Deer Isle was like ____
20. White Mountains are in this state

Travels With Charley Fill In The Blanks 2 Answer Key

QUIXOTE	1. Rocinante was named for Don ___'s horse
MIND	2. Texas is a state of ____, according to Mr. Steinbeck
MOBILE	3. These homes were revolutionary
SALINAS	4. Mr. Steinbeck's home town in California
ELEYNE	5. Fair ___; the boat
CHILD	6. The Bad Lands seemed like the work of an evil ____
RABIES	7. Charley didn't have his certificate of vaccination for this
GLACIERS	8. Responsible for wiping out most of the redwood trees
TRAVELS	9. ____ With Charley
CHICAGO	10. Place where Mr. Steinbeck's wife met him to visit
HARBOR	11. Sag ___; starting point of the trip
ORLEANS	12. New ___; place where the Cheerleaders demonstrated
WIFE	13. The boat was named for Steinbeck's
ALLERGIC	14. Charley was ___ to insecticides
CANUCKS	15. Maine's migrant farmers
TRIP	16. You don't take one, one takes you
REDWOOD	17. These trees cause wonder & respect in man
ROBBIE	18. He wanted to be a hairdresser
AVALON	19. Deer Isle was like ____
MAINE	20. White Mountains are in this state

Travels With Charley Fill In The Blanks 3

_____
_____
_____
_____
_____
_____
_____
_____
_____
_____
_____
_____
_____
_____
_____
_____
_____
_____
_____
_____

1. The boat was named for Steinbeck's
2. Two cans of dog food were left for them
3. Desert Mr. Steinbeck and Charley crossed
4. Sag ___; starting point of the trip
5. They have their own language, according to Mr. Steinbeck
6. Wisconsin ___; formed by ice during the Ice Age
7. Charley didn't have his certificate of vaccination for this
8. Lonesome ___; previous occupant of the hotel room
9. New ___; place where the Cheerleaders demonstrated
10. He wanted to be a hairdresser
11. Only state to enter the union by treaty
12. White Mountains are in this state
13. Deer Isle was like ____
14. Charley was ___ to insecticides
15. Minneapolis & St. Paul are the ___ Cities
16. Kind of sermon in Vermont: ___ & Brimstone
17. Rocinante was named for Don ___'s horse
18. Group of white women gathered at school to protest desegregation
19. The Bad Lands seemed like the work of an evil ____
20. Texas is a state of ____, according to Mr. Steinbeck

Travels With Charley Fill In The Blanks 3 Answer Key

WIFE	1. The boat was named for Steinbeck's
COYOTES	2. Two cans of dog food were left for them
MOJAVE	3. Desert Mr. Steinbeck and Charley crossed
HARBOR	4. Sag ___; starting point of the trip
TRUCKERS	5. They have their own language, according to Mr. Steinbeck
DELLS	6. Wisconsin ___; formed by ice during the Ice Age
RABIES	7. Charley didn't have his certificate of vaccination for this
HARRY	8. Lonesome ___; previous occupant of the hotel room
ORLEANS	9. New ___; place where the Cheerleaders demonstrated
ROBBIE	10. He wanted to be a hairdresser
TEXAS	11. Only state to enter the union by treaty
MAINE	12. White Mountains are in this state
AVALON	13. Deer Isle was like ____
ALLERGIC	14. Charley was ___ to insecticides
TWIN	15. Minneapolis & St. Paul are the ___ Cities
FIRE	16. Kind of sermon in Vermont: ___ & Brimstone
QUIXOTE	17. Rocinante was named for Don ___'s horse
CHEERLEADERS	18. Group of white women gathered at school to protest desegregation
CHILD	19. The Bad Lands seemed like the work of an evil ____
MIND	20. Texas is a state of ____, according to Mr. Steinbeck

Travels With Charley Fill In The Blanks 4

_____
_____
_____
_____
_____
_____
_____
_____
_____
_____
_____
_____
_____
_____
_____
_____
_____
_____
_____
_____

1. Desert Mr. Steinbeck and Charley crossed
2. This river, according to Mr. Steinbeck, should have been the east-west middle of the country
3. You don't take one, one takes you
4. Author
5. These homes were revolutionary
6. Near the end of the book, Mr. Steinbeck gave reasons why he couldn't find the ___ about the country
7. Texas is a state of ____, according to Mr. Steinbeck
8. He wanted to be a hairdresser
9. Wisconsin ___; formed by ice during the Ice Age
10. Responsible for wiping out most of the redwood trees
11. Mr. Steinbeck used Charley as this with strangers
12. Maine's migrant farmers
13. Minneapolis & St. Paul are the ___ Cities
14. Charley was ___ to insecticides
15. Hotel in Chicago: ___ East
16. Lonesome ___; previous occupant of the hotel room
17. Deer Isle was like ____
18. They have their own language, according to Mr. Steinbeck
19. Going somewhere with a direction in mind but not caring if you get there or not
20. Sag ___; starting point of the trip

Travels With Charley Fill In The Blanks 4 Answer Key

MOJAVE	1. Desert Mr. Steinbeck and Charley crossed
MISSOURI	2. This river, according to Mr. Steinbeck, should have been the east-west middle of the country
TRIP	3. You don't take one, one takes you
STEINBECK	4. Author
MOBILE	5. These homes were revolutionary
TRUTH	6. Near the end of the book, Mr. Steinbeck gave reasons why he couldn't find the ___ about the country
MIND	7. Texas is a state of ____, according to Mr. Steinbeck
ROBBIE	8. He wanted to be a hairdresser
DELLS	9. Wisconsin ___; formed by ice during the Ice Age
GLACIERS	10. Responsible for wiping out most of the redwood trees
ICEBREAKER	11. Mr. Steinbeck used Charley as this with strangers
CANUCKS	12. Maine's migrant farmers
TWIN	13. Minneapolis & St. Paul are the ___ Cities
ALLERGIC	14. Charley was ___ to insecticides
AMBASSADOR	15. Hotel in Chicago: ___ East
HARRY	16. Lonesome ___; previous occupant of the hotel room
AVALON	17. Deer Isle was like ____
TRUCKERS	18. They have their own language, according to Mr. Steinbeck
VACILANDO	19. Going somewhere with a direction in mind but not caring if you get there or not
HARBOR	20. Sag ___; starting point of the trip

Travels With Charley Matching 1

___ 1. POTATO A. Charley wanted to fight them at Yellowstone
___ 2. COFFEE B. Topic of family arguments
___ 3. THOUGHT C. Mr. Steinbeck wanted to see these crops in Maine
___ 4. HARRY D. The poodle; companion to Mr. Steinbeck
___ 5. MONTANA E. Maine's migrant farmers
___ 6. CANUCKS F. Mr. Steinbeck used Charley as this with strangers
___ 7. TEXAS G. Responsible for wiping out most of the redwood trees
___ 8. ICEBREAKER H. This country wouldn't let Charley in
___ 9. MIND I. Lonesome ___; previous occupant of the hotel room
___ 10. MOJAVE J. Going somewhere with a direction in mind but not caring if you get there or not
___ 11. BEARS K. In this state Mr. Steinbeck realized his trip had ended
___ 12. ALLERGIC L. Texas is a state of ____, according to Mr. Steinbeck
___ 13. CHARLEY M. Two cans of dog food were left for them
___ 14. MAINE N. White Mountains are in this state
___ 15. VIRGINIA O. Charley was ___ to insecticides
___ 16. GLACIERS P. They have their own language, according to Mr. Steinbeck
___ 17. POLITICS Q. New ___; place where the Cheerleaders demonstrated
___ 18. ORLEANS R. It is the great get-together symbol
___ 19. CANADA S. Author
___ 20. STEINBECK T. Desert Mr. Steinbeck and Charley crossed
___ 21. VACILANDO U. A man has to have feelings and then words before he can come close to this
___ 22. TRUCKERS V. The truck
___ 23. ROCINANTE W. State Mr. Steinbeck considered a great splash of grandeur
___ 24. CHICAGO X. Place where Mr. Steinbeck's wife met him to visit
___ 25. COYOTES Y. Only state to enter the union by treaty

Travels With Charley Matching 1 Answer Key

C - 1. POTATO	A. Charley wanted to fight them at Yellowstone
R - 2. COFFEE	B. Topic of family arguments
U - 3. THOUGHT	C. Mr. Steinbeck wanted to see these crops in Maine
I - 4. HARRY	D. The poodle; companion to Mr. Steinbeck
W - 5. MONTANA	E. Maine's migrant farmers
E - 6. CANUCKS	F. Mr. Steinbeck used Charley as this with strangers
Y - 7. TEXAS	G. Responsible for wiping out most of the redwood trees
F - 8. ICEBREAKER	H. This country wouldn't let Charley in
L - 9. MIND	I. Lonesome ___; previous occupant of the hotel room
T - 10. MOJAVE	J. Going somewhere with a direction in mind but not caring if you get there or not
A - 11. BEARS	K. In this state Mr. Steinbeck realized his trip had ended
O - 12. ALLERGIC	L. Texas is a state of ____, according to Mr. Steinbeck
D - 13. CHARLEY	M. Two cans of dog food were left for them
N - 14. MAINE	N. White Mountains are in this state
K - 15. VIRGINIA	O. Charley was ___ to insecticides
G - 16. GLACIERS	P. They have their own language, according to Mr. Steinbeck
B - 17. POLITICS	Q. New ___; place where the Cheerleaders demonstrated
Q - 18. ORLEANS	R. It is the great get-together symbol
H - 19. CANADA	S. Author
S - 20. STEINBECK	T. Desert Mr. Steinbeck and Charley crossed
J - 21. VACILANDO	U. A man has to have feelings and then words before he can come close to this
P - 22. TRUCKERS	V. The truck
V - 23. ROCINANTE	W. State Mr. Steinbeck considered a great splash of grandeur
X - 24. CHICAGO	X. Place where Mr. Steinbeck's wife met him to visit
M - 25. COYOTES	Y. Only state to enter the union by treaty

Travels With Charley Matching 2

___ 1. AVALON   A. Charley was ___ to insecticides
___ 2. TRIP   B. Fair ___; the boat
___ 3. AMBASSADOR   C. Sag ___; starting point of the trip
___ 4. TEXAS   D. Topic of family arguments
___ 5. ROBBIE   E. In this state Mr. Steinbeck realized his trip had ended
___ 6. DELLS   F. The boat was named for Steinbeck's
___ 7. BEARS   G. New ___; place where the Cheerleaders demonstrated
___ 8. TRUTH   H. Kind of sermon in Vermont: ___ & Brimstone
___ 9. VIRGINIA   I. Two cans of dog food were left for them
___10. THOUGHT   J. Wisconsin ___; formed by ice during the Ice Age
___11. ELEYNE   K. Deer Isle was like ___
___12. POTATO   L. Near the end of the book, Mr. Steinbeck gave reasons why he couldn't find the ___ about the country
___13. HARBOR   M. Mr. Steinbeck wanted to see these crops in Maine
___14. ALLERGIC   N. Maine's migrant farmers
___15. COFFEE   O. Rocinante was named for Don ___'s horse
___16. POLITICS   P. Hotel in Chicago: ___ East
___17. GLACIERS   Q. Only state to enter the union by treaty
___18. ORLEANS   R. Charley wanted to fight them at Yellowstone
___19. WIFE   S. A man has to have feelings and then words before he can come close to this
___20. COYOTES   T. Lonesome ___; previous occupant of the hotel room
___21. FIRE   U. You don't take one, one takes you
___22. ICEBREAKER   V. Mr. Steinbeck used Charley as this with strangers
___23. QUIXOTE   W. He wanted to be a hairdresser
___24. CANUCKS   X. It is the great get-together symbol
___25. HARRY   Y. Responsible for wiping out most of the redwood trees

Travels With Charley Matching 2 Answer Key

K - 1. AVALON	A. Charley was ___ to insecticides
U - 2. TRIP	B. Fair ___; the boat
P - 3. AMBASSADOR	C. Sag ___; starting point of the trip
Q - 4. TEXAS	D. Topic of family arguments
W - 5. ROBBIE	E. In this state Mr. Steinbeck realized his trip had ended
J - 6. DELLS	F. The boat was named for Steinbeck's
R - 7. BEARS	G. New ___; place where the Cheerleaders demonstrated
L - 8. TRUTH	H. Kind of sermon in Vermont: ___ & Brimstone
E - 9. VIRGINIA	I. Two cans of dog food were left for them
S - 10. THOUGHT	J. Wisconsin ___; formed by ice during the Ice Age
B - 11. ELEYNE	K. Deer Isle was like ___
M - 12. POTATO	L. Near the end of the book, Mr. Steinbeck gave reasons why he couldn't find the ___ about the country
C - 13. HARBOR	M. Mr. Steinbeck wanted to see these crops in Maine
A - 14. ALLERGIC	N. Maine's migrant farmers
X - 15. COFFEE	O. Rocinante was named for Don ___'s horse
D - 16. POLITICS	P. Hotel in Chicago: ___ East
Y - 17. GLACIERS	Q. Only state to enter the union by treaty
G - 18. ORLEANS	R. Charley wanted to fight them at Yellowstone
F - 19. WIFE	S. A man has to have feelings and then words before he can come close to this
I - 20. COYOTES	T. Lonesome ___; previous occupant of the hotel room
H - 21. FIRE	U. You don't take one, one takes you
V - 22. ICEBREAKER	V. Mr. Steinbeck used Charley as this with strangers
O - 23. QUIXOTE	W. He wanted to be a hairdresser
N - 24. CANUCKS	X. It is the great get-together symbol
T - 25. HARRY	Y. Responsible for wiping out most of the redwood trees

Travels With Charley Matching 3

___ 1. MISSOURI
___ 2. TRAVELS
___ 3. FIRE
___ 4. CANADA
___ 5. REDWOOD
___ 6. MAINE
___ 7. TRIP
___ 8. CHILD
___ 9. MIND
___10. DELLS
___11. WIFE
___12. VIRGINIA
___13. CHEERLEADERS
___14. COYOTES
___15. TWIN
___16. ALLERGIC
___17. SALINAS
___18. VACILANDO
___19. COFFEE
___20. TEXAS
___21. QUIXOTE
___22. ICEBREAKER
___23. STEINBECK
___24. TRUTH
___25. BEARS

A. The Bad Lands seemed like the work of an evil ____
B. Going somewhere with a direction in mind but not caring if you get there or not
C. This river, according to Mr. Steinbeck, should have been the east-west middle of the country
D. In this state Mr. Steinbeck realized his trip had ended
E. Mr. Steinbeck's home town in California
F. Only state to enter the union by treaty
G. This country wouldn't let Charley in
H. Minneapolis & St. Paul are the ___ Cities
I. White Mountains are in this state
J. Rocinante was named for Don ___'s horse
K. Kind of sermon in Vermont: ___ & Brimstone
L. Author
M. The boat was named for Steinbeck's
N. Charley was ___ to insecticides
O. Near the end of the book, Mr. Steinbeck gave reasons why he couldn't find the ___ about the country
P. Charley wanted to fight them at Yellowstone
Q. You don't take one, one takes you
R. ____ With Charley
S. Wisconsin ___; formed by ice during the Ice Age
T. Group of white women gathered at school to protest desegregation
U. Mr. Steinbeck used Charley as this with strangers
V. It is the great get-together symbol
W. These trees cause wonder & respect in man
X. Texas is a state of ____, according to Mr. Steinbeck
Y. Two cans of dog food were left for them

Travels With Charley Matching 3 Answer Key

C - 1. MISSOURI	A. The Bad Lands seemed like the work of an evil ____
R - 2. TRAVELS	B. Going somewhere with a direction in mind but not caring if you get there or not
K - 3. FIRE	C. This river, according to Mr. Steinbeck, should have been the east-west middle of the country
G - 4. CANADA	D. In this state Mr. Steinbeck realized his trip had ended
W - 5. REDWOOD	E. Mr. Steinbeck's home town in California
I - 6. MAINE	F. Only state to enter the union by treaty
Q - 7. TRIP	G. This country wouldn't let Charley in
A - 8. CHILD	H. Minneapolis & St. Paul are the ____ Cities
X - 9. MIND	I. White Mountains are in this state
S - 10. DELLS	J. Rocinante was named for Don ____'s horse
M - 11. WIFE	K. Kind of sermon in Vermont: ____ & Brimstone
D - 12. VIRGINIA	L. Author
T - 13. CHEERLEADERS	M. The boat was named for Steinbeck's
Y - 14. COYOTES	N. Charley was ____ to insecticides
H - 15. TWIN	O. Near the end of the book, Mr. Steinbeck gave reasons why he couldn't find the ____ about the country
N - 16. ALLERGIC	P. Charley wanted to fight them at Yellowstone
E - 17. SALINAS	Q. You don't take one, one takes you
B - 18. VACILANDO	R. ____ With Charley
V - 19. COFFEE	S. Wisconsin ____; formed by ice during the Ice Age
F - 20. TEXAS	T. Group of white women gathered at school to protest desegregation
J - 21. QUIXOTE	U. Mr. Steinbeck used Charley as this with strangers
U - 22. ICEBREAKER	V. It is the great get-together symbol
L - 23. STEINBECK	W. These trees cause wonder & respect in man
O - 24. TRUTH	X. Texas is a state of ____, according to Mr. Steinbeck
P - 25. BEARS	Y. Two cans of dog food were left for them

Travels With Charley Matching 4

___ 1. VIRGINIA A. In this state Mr. Steinbeck realized his trip had ended
___ 2. DELLS B. Charley wanted to fight them at Yellowstone
___ 3. CHARLEY C. Mr. Steinbeck's home town in California
___ 4. MOBILE D. Author
___ 5. ORLEANS E. The boat was named for Steinbeck's
___ 6. COYOTES F. The east-west middle of the country was in ___, ND
___ 7. GLACIERS G. The poodle; companion to Mr. Steinbeck
___ 8. TRUCKERS H. Texas is a state of ____, according to Mr. Steinbeck
___ 9. SALINAS I. They have their own language, according to Mr. Steinbeck
___ 10. BEARS J. Hotel in Chicago: ___ East
___ 11. MOJAVE K. Desert Mr. Steinbeck and Charley crossed
___ 12. MAINE L. Maine's migrant farmers
___ 13. TEXAS M. Charley didn't have his certificate of vaccination for this
___ 14. TRUTH N. It is the great get-together symbol
___ 15. MIND O. Going somewhere with a direction in mind but not caring if you get there or not
___ 16. CANUCKS P. White Mountains are in this state
___ 17. ELEYNE Q. New ___; place where the Cheerleaders demonstrated
___ 18. RABIES R. Near the end of the book, Mr. Steinbeck gave reasons why he couldn't find the ___ about the country
___ 19. WIFE S. Wisconsin ___; formed by ice during the Ice Age
___ 20. STEINBECK T. Two cans of dog food were left for them
___ 21. FARGO U. Fair ___; the boat
___ 22. VACILANDO V. You don't take one, one takes you
___ 23. COFFEE W. Responsible for wiping out most of the redwood trees
___ 24. TRIP X. These homes were revolutionary
___ 25. AMBASSADOR Y. Only state to enter the union by treaty

Travels With Charley Matching 4 Answer Key

A - 1. VIRGINIA	A. In this state Mr. Steinbeck realized his trip had ended
S - 2. DELLS	B. Charley wanted to fight them at Yellowstone
G - 3. CHARLEY	C. Mr. Steinbeck's home town in California
X - 4. MOBILE	D. Author
Q - 5. ORLEANS	E. The boat was named for Steinbeck's
T - 6. COYOTES	F. The east-west middle of the country was in ___, ND
W - 7. GLACIERS	G. The poodle; companion to Mr. Steinbeck
I - 8. TRUCKERS	H. Texas is a state of ____, according to Mr. Steinbeck
C - 9. SALINAS	I. They have their own language, according to Mr. Steinbeck
B - 10. BEARS	J. Hotel in Chicago: ___ East
K - 11. MOJAVE	K. Desert Mr. Steinbeck and Charley crossed
P - 12. MAINE	L. Maine's migrant farmers
Y - 13. TEXAS	M. Charley didn't have his certificate of vaccination for this
R - 14. TRUTH	N. It is the great get-together symbol
H - 15. MIND	O. Going somewhere with a direction in mind but not caring if you get there or not
L - 16. CANUCKS	P. White Mountains are in this state
U - 17. ELEYNE	Q. New ___; place where the Cheerleaders demonstrated
M - 18. RABIES	R. Near the end of the book, Mr. Steinbeck gave reasons why he couldn't find the ___ about the country
E - 19. WIFE	S. Wisconsin ___; formed by ice during the Ice Age
D - 20. STEINBECK	T. Two cans of dog food were left for them
F - 21. FARGO	U. Fair ___; the boat
O - 22. VACILANDO	V. You don't take one, one takes you
N - 23. COFFEE	W. Responsible for wiping out most of the redwood trees
V - 24. TRIP	X. These homes were revolutionary
J - 25. AMBASSADOR	Y. Only state to enter the union by treaty

Travels With Charley Magic Squares 1

Match the definition with the vocabulary word. Put your answers in the magic squares below. When your answers are correct, all columns and rows will add to the same number.

A. THOUGHT
B. TEXAS
C. FIRE
D. FARGO
E. TRUCKERS
F. ICEBREAKER
G. STEINBECK
H. CHILD
I. VIRGINIA
J. GLACIERS
K. CANUCKS
L. SALINAS
M. CHARLEY
N. COFFEE
O. ROCINANTE
P. CHICAGO

1. The Bad Lands seemed like the work of an evil ____
2. The poodle; companion to Mr. Steinbeck
3. Only state to enter the union by treaty
4. Maine's migrant farmers
5. Responsible for wiping out most of the redwood trees
6. Kind of sermon in Vermont: ___ & Brimstone
7. Place where Mr. Steinbeck's wife met him to visit
8. They have their own language, according to Mr. Steinbeck
9. The truck
10. Mr. Steinbeck used Charley as this with strangers
11. In this state Mr. Steinbeck realized his trip had ended
12. The east-west middle of the country was in ___, ND
13. A man has to have feelings and then words before he can come close to this
14. Mr. Steinbeck's home town in California
15. Author
16. It is the great get-together symbol

A=	B=	C=	D=
E=	F=	G=	H=
I=	J=	K=	L=
M=	N=	O=	P=

Travels With Charley Magic Squares 1 Answer Key

Match the definition with the vocabulary word. Put your answers in the magic squares below. When your answers are correct, all columns and rows will add to the same number.

A. THOUGHT
B. TEXAS
C. FIRE
D. FARGO
E. TRUCKERS
F. ICEBREAKER
G. STEINBECK
H. CHILD
I. VIRGINIA
J. GLACIERS
K. CANUCKS
L. SALINAS
M. CHARLEY
N. COFFEE
O. ROCINANTE
P. CHICAGO

1. The Bad Lands seemed like the work of an evil ____
2. The poodle; companion to Mr. Steinbeck
3. Only state to enter the union by treaty
4. Maine's migrant farmers
5. Responsible for wiping out most of the redwood trees
6. Kind of sermon in Vermont: ___ & Brimstone
7. Place where Mr. Steinbeck's wife met him to visit
8. They have their own language, according to Mr. Steinbeck
9. The truck
10. Mr. Steinbeck used Charley as this with strangers
11. In this state Mr. Steinbeck realized his trip had ended
12. The east-west middle of the country was in ___, ND
13. A man has to have feelings and then words before he can come close to this
14. Mr. Steinbeck's home town in California
15. Author
16. It is the great get-together symbol

A=13	B=3	C=6	D=12
E=8	F=10	G=15	H=1
I=11	J=5	K=4	L=14
M=2	N=16	O=9	P=7

Travels With Charley Magic Squares 2

Match the definition with the vocabulary word. Put your answers in the magic squares below. When your answers are correct, all columns and rows will add to the same number.

A. THOUGHT
B. CHEERLEADERS
C. QUIXOTE
D. CHICAGO
E. CHARLEY
F. RABIES
G. POLITICS
H. TEXAS
I. HARBOR
J. MAINE
K. FIRE
L. ELEYNE
M. TRAVELS
N. POTATO
O. MOJAVE
P. COFFEE

1. Only state to enter the union by treaty
2. A man has to have feelings and then words before he can come close to this
3. Group of white women gathered at school to protest desegregation
4. Topic of family arguments
5. White Mountains are in this state
6. Desert Mr. Steinbeck and Charley crossed
7. It is the great get-together symbol
8. Sag ___; starting point of the trip
9. Kind of sermon in Vermont: ___ & Brimstone
10. Mr. Steinbeck wanted to see these crops in Maine
11. ___ With Charley
12. Fair ___; the boat
13. The poodle; companion to Mr. Steinbeck
14. Place where Mr. Steinbeck's wife met him to visit
15. Rocinante was named for Don ___'s horse
16. Charley didn't have his certificate of vaccination for this

A=	B=	C=	D=
E=	F=	G=	H=
I=	J=	K=	L=
M=	N=	O=	P=

Travels With Charley Magic Squares 2 Answer Key

Match the definition with the vocabulary word. Put your answers in the magic squares below. When your answers are correct, all columns and rows will add to the same number.

A. THOUGHT
B. CHEERLEADERS
C. QUIXOTE
D. CHICAGO
E. CHARLEY
F. RABIES

G. POLITICS
H. TEXAS
I. HARBOR
J. MAINE
K. FIRE
L. ELEYNE

M. TRAVELS
N. POTATO
O. MOJAVE
P. COFFEE

1. Only state to enter the union by treaty
2. A man has to have feelings and then words before he can come close to this
3. Group of white women gathered at school to protest desegregation
4. Topic of family arguments
5. White Mountains are in this state
6. Desert Mr. Steinbeck and Charley crossed
7. It is the great get-together symbol
8. Sag ___; starting point of the trip
9. Kind of sermon in Vermont: ___ & Brimstone
10. Mr. Steinbeck wanted to see these crops in Maine
11. ___ With Charley
12. Fair ___; the boat
13. The poodle; companion to Mr. Steinbeck
14. Place where Mr. Steinbeck's wife met him to visit
15. Rocinante was named for Don ___'s horse
16. Charley didn't have his certificate of vaccination for this

A=2	B=3	C=15	D=14
E=13	F=16	G=4	H=1
I=8	J=5	K=9	L=12
M=11	N=10	O=6	P=7

Travels With Charley Magic Squares 3

Match the definition with the vocabulary word. Put your answers in the magic squares below. When your answers are correct, all columns and rows will add to the same number.

A. THOUGHT
B. AVALON
C. FIRE
D. SALINAS
E. AMBASSADOR
F. ORLEANS
G. TEXAS
H. HARBOR
I. ICEBREAKER
J. VACILANDO
K. MOBILE
L. ELEYNE
M. CHILD
N. POLITICS
O. CHICAGO
P. TRIP

1. Deer Isle was like ____
2. Only state to enter the union by treaty
3. These homes were revolutionary
4. Topic of family arguments
5. The Bad Lands seemed like the work of an evil ____
6. Fair ___; the boat
7. Sag ___; starting point of the trip
8. A man has to have feelings and then words before he can come close to this
9. You don't take one, one takes you
10. Mr. Steinbeck used Charley as this with strangers
11. Hotel in Chicago: ___ East
12. Mr. Steinbeck's home town in California
13. Kind of sermon in Vermont: ___ & Brimstone
14. New ___; place where the Cheerleaders demonstrated
15. Going somewhere with a direction in mind but not caring if you get there or not
16. Place where Mr. Steinbeck's wife met him to visit

A=	B=	C=	D=
E=	F=	G=	H=
I=	J=	K=	L=
M=	N=	O=	P=

Travels With Charley Magic Squares 3 Answer Key

Match the definition with the vocabulary word. Put your answers in the magic squares below. When your answers are correct, all columns and rows will add to the same number.

A. THOUGHT
B. AVALON
C. FIRE
D. SALINAS
E. AMBASSADOR
F. ORLEANS
G. TEXAS
H. HARBOR
I. ICEBREAKER
J. VACILANDO
K. MOBILE
L. ELEYNE
M. CHILD
N. POLITICS
O. CHICAGO
P. TRIP

1. Deer Isle was like ____
2. Only state to enter the union by treaty
3. These homes were revolutionary
4. Topic of family arguments
5. The Bad Lands seemed like the work of an evil ____
6. Fair ____; the boat
7. Sag ____; starting point of the trip
8. A man has to have feelings and then words before he can come close to this
9. You don't take one, one takes you
10. Mr. Steinbeck used Charley as this with strangers
11. Hotel in Chicago: ____ East
12. Mr. Steinbeck's home town in California
13. Kind of sermon in Vermont: ____ & Brimstone
14. New ____; place where the Cheerleaders demonstrated
15. Going somewhere with a direction in mind but not caring if you get there or not
16. Place where Mr. Steinbeck's wife met him to visit

A=8	B=1	C=13	D=12
E=11	F=14	G=2	H=7
I=10	J=15	K=3	L=6
M=5	N=4	O=16	P=9

Travels With Charley Magic Squares 4

Match the definition with the vocabulary word. Put your answers in the magic squares below. When your answers are correct, all columns and rows will add to the same number.

A. TRUCKERS
B. TEXAS
C. REDWOOD
D. HARRY
E. POLITICS
F. AVALON
G. HARBOR
H. TRAVELS
I. CHILD
J. AMBASSADOR
K. MISSOURI
L. POTATO
M. BEARS
N. ROBBIE
O. QUIXOTE
P. ICEBREAKER

1. These trees cause wonder & respect in man
2. Hotel in Chicago: ___ East
3. Deer Isle was like ____
4. Rocinante was named for Don ___'s horse
5. Mr. Steinbeck used Charley as this with strangers
6. Topic of family arguments
7. The Bad Lands seemed like the work of an evil ____
8. Lonesome ___; previous occupant of the hotel room
9. Charley wanted to fight them at Yellowstone
10. ____ With Charley
11. Mr. Steinbeck wanted to see these crops in Maine
12. They have their own language, according to Mr. Steinbeck
13. Only state to enter the union by treaty
14. This river, according to Mr. Steinbeck, should have been the east-west middle of the country
15. Sag ___; starting point of the trip
16. He wanted to be a hairdresser

A=	B=	C=	D=
E=	F=	G=	H=
I=	J=	K=	L=
M=	N=	O=	P=

Travels With Charley Magic Squares 4 Answer Key

Match the definition with the vocabulary word. Put your answers in the magic squares below. When your answers are correct, all columns and rows will add to the same number.

A. TRUCKERS
B. TEXAS
C. REDWOOD
D. HARRY
E. POLITICS
F. AVALON
G. HARBOR
H. TRAVELS
I. CHILD
J. AMBASSADOR
K. MISSOURI
L. POTATO
M. BEARS
N. ROBBIE
O. QUIXOTE
P. ICEBREAKER

1. These trees cause wonder & respect in man
2. Hotel in Chicago: ___ East
3. Deer Isle was like ___
4. Rocinante was named for Don ___'s horse
5. Mr. Steinbeck used Charley as this with strangers
6. Topic of family arguments
7. The Bad Lands seemed like the work of an evil ___
8. Lonesome ___; previous occupant of the hotel room
9. Charley wanted to fight them at Yellowstone
10. ___ With Charley
11. Mr. Steinbeck wanted to see these crops in Maine
12. They have their own language, according to Mr. Steinbeck
13. Only state to enter the union by treaty
14. This river, according to Mr. Steinbeck, should have been the east-west middle of the country
15. Sag ___; starting point of the trip
16. He wanted to be a hairdresser

A=12	B=13	C=1	D=8
E=6	F=3	G=15	H=10
I=7	J=2	K=14	L=11
M=9	N=16	O=4	P=5

Travels With Charley Word Search 1

```
M L P I R T T L M Y S E T O Y O C M
O O W T F E G R R I R B R D E T I W
J C N R H E D R A I N X A N L R C M
A F H T L O A W F V G D B A R U E C
V S A I A H U P O S E F I L A T B W
E X B R L N N G C O Y L E I H H R N
F O Q V G D A I H H D M S C C C E N
M W G G X O T G C T A E H A B O A F
Q V I R G I N I A S Q R L V S F K C
S A N I L A S I C M T U B L Z F E F
X R Z O C D S R V A D O I O S E R W
L W P B I V K U P Y N G P X R E S Q
C S I H G C C O R T W A Z X O D A T
C C Z F R B U S X R W C D M B T X P
S O R L E A N S R O C I N A N T E M
V V T A L W A I R C T H N I F S T D
B Z R L L Y C M H V J C E N Y E L E
W S A V A L O N R O B B I E C K W W
```

A man has to have feelings and then words before he can come close to this (7)

Charley didn't have his certificate of vaccination for this (6)

Charley wanted to fight them at Yellowstone (5)

Charley was ___ to insecticides (8)

Deer Isle was like ____ (6)

Desert Mr. Steinbeck and Charley crossed (6)

Fair ___; the boat (6)

Going somewhere with a direction in mind but not caring if you get there or not (9)

He wanted to be a hairdresser (6)

In this state Mr. Steinbeck realized his trip had ended (8)

It is the great get-together symbol (6)

Kind of sermon in Vermont: ___ & Brimstone (4)

Lonesome ___; previous occupant of the hotel room (5)

Maine's migrant farmers (7)

Minneapolis & St. Paul are the ___ Cities (4)

Mr. Steinbeck used Charley as this with strangers (10)

Mr. Steinbeck's home town in California (7)

Near the end of the book, Mr. Steinbeck gave reasons why he couldn't find the ___ about the country

New ___; place where the Cheerleaders demonstrated (7)

Only state to enter the union by treaty (5)

Place where Mr. Steinbeck's wife met him to visit (7)

Rocinante was named for Don ___'s horse (7)

Sag ___; starting point of the trip (6)

State Mr. Steinbeck considered a great splash of grandeur (7)

Texas is a state of ____, according to Mr. Steinbeck (4)

The Bad Lands seemed like the work of an evil ____ (5)

The boat was named for Steinbeck's (4)

The east-west middle of the country was in ___, ND (5)

The poodle; companion to Mr. Steinbeck (7)

The truck (9)

These homes were revolutionary (6)

These trees cause wonder & respect in man (7)

This country wouldn't let Charley in (6)

This river, according to Mr. Steinbeck, should have been the east-west middle of the country (8)

Topic of family arguments (8)

Two cans of dog food were left for them (7)

White Mountains are in this state (5)

Wisconsin ___; formed by ice during the Ice Age (5)

You don't take one, one takes you (4)

____ With Charley (7)

Travels With Charley Word Search 1 Answer Key

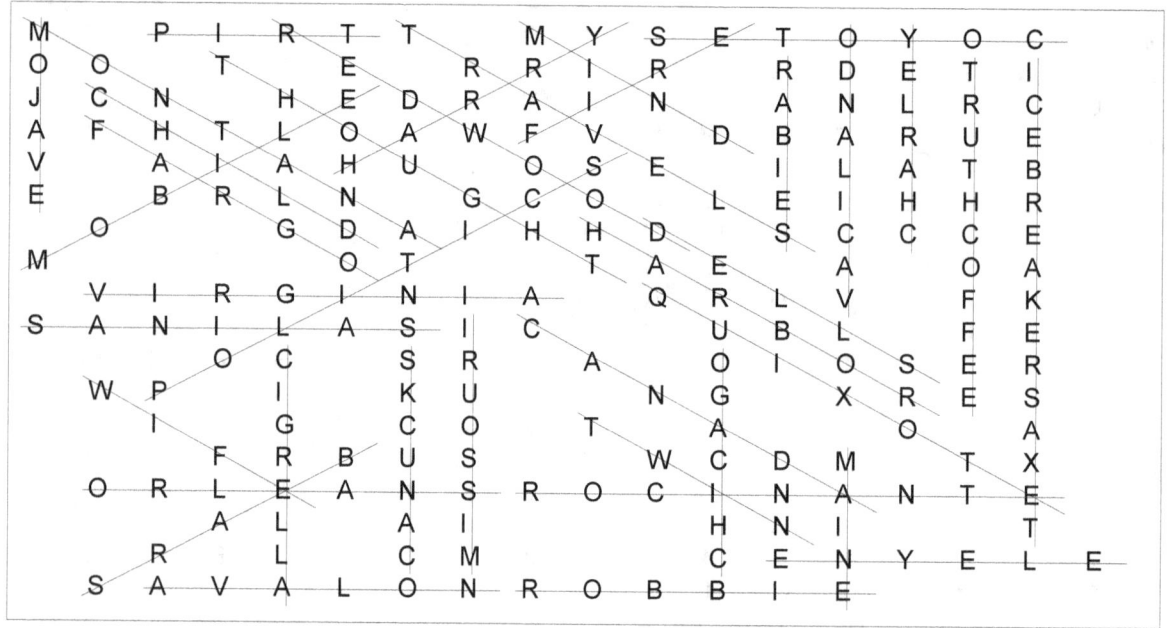

A man has to have feelings and then words before he can come close to this (7)
Charley didn't have his certificate of vaccination for this (6)
Charley wanted to fight them at Yellowstone (5)
Charley was ___ to insecticides (8)
Deer Isle was like ____ (6)
Desert Mr. Steinbeck and Charley crossed (6)
Fair ___; the boat (6)
Going somewhere with a direction in mind but not caring if you get there or not (9)
He wanted to be a hairdresser (6)
In this state Mr. Steinbeck realized his trip had ended (8)
It is the great get-together symbol (6)
Kind of sermon in Vermont: ___ & Brimstone (4)
Lonesome ___; previous occupant of the hotel room (5)
Maine's migrant farmers (7)
Minneapolis & St. Paul are the ___ Cities (4)
Mr. Steinbeck used Charley as this with strangers (10)
Mr. Steinbeck's home town in California (7)
Near the end of the book, Mr. Steinbeck gave reasons why he couldn't find the ___ about the country
New ___; place where the Cheerleaders demonstrated (7)

Only state to enter the union by treaty (5)
Place where Mr. Steinbeck's wife met him to visit (7)
Rocinante was named for Don ___'s horse (7)
Sag ___; starting point of the trip (6)
State Mr. Steinbeck considered a great splash of grandeur (7)
Texas is a state of ____, according to Mr. Steinbeck (4)
The Bad Lands seemed like the work of an evil ____ (5)
The boat was named for Steinbeck's (4)
The east-west middle of the country was in ___, ND (5)
The poodle; companion to Mr. Steinbeck (7)
The truck (9)
These homes were revolutionary (6)
These trees cause wonder & respect in man (7)
This country wouldn't let Charley in (6)
This river, according to Mr. Steinbeck, should have been the east-west middle of the country (8)
Topic of family arguments (8)
Two cans of dog food were left for them (7)
White Mountains are in this state (5)
Wisconsin ___; formed by ice during the Ice Age (5)
You don't take one, one takes you (4)
____ With Charley (7)

Travels With Charley Word Search 2

```
H N J K M S T A R O C I N A N T E B
P A X D I J T H L S L H F V G L A J
O O R J S T E X O L A T I W S I M G
L R D B S S X B P U E L C C N L D N
I L E C O M A I N E G R I I A V S N
T E L A U R S T W Y Y H G N B G S B
I A L N R K C Z R K W R T I A Z O E
C N S A I X O Y G A I D N Y C S T R
S S O D Q P Y D W V V L J K Z O O W
B G G A O M O B I L E E W H X D J N
M Z R T Z W T B F R F Z L I A G T R
A V A L O N E L E Y N E U S T R I P
M T F C J I S D M A E Q S L U A H C
O I Q K B R W D K F R A M T R B A J
T Z N B V O L F F Y B S H X F I R G
W H O D O I L O I M O J A V E E R K
I R N D H C H A R L E Y T F S Y G
N V A C I L A N D O E C A N U C K S
```

A man has to have feelings and then words before he can come close to this (7)
Charley didn't have his certificate of vaccination for this (6)
Charley wanted to fight them at Yellowstone (5)
Charley was ___ to insecticides (8)
Deer Isle was like _____ (6)
Desert Mr. Steinbeck and Charley crossed (6)
Fair ___; the boat (6)
Going somewhere with a direction in mind but not caring if you get there or not (9)
He wanted to be a hairdresser (6)
Hotel in Chicago: ___ East (10)
In this state Mr. Steinbeck realized his trip had ended (8)
It is the great get-together symbol (6)
Kind of sermon in Vermont: ___ & Brimstone (4)
Lonesome ___; previous occupant of the hotel room (5)
Maine's migrant farmers (7)
Minneapolis & St. Paul are the ___ Cities (4)
Mr. Steinbeck wanted to see these crops in Maine (6)
Mr. Steinbeck's home town in California (7)
Near the end of the book, Mr. Steinbeck gave reasons why he couldn't find the ___ about the country
New ___; place where the Cheerleaders demonstrated (7)
Only state to enter the union by treaty (5)
Place where Mr. Steinbeck's wife met him to visit (7)
Rocinante was named for Don ___'s horse (7)
Sag ___; starting point of the trip (6)
Texas is a state of ____, according to Mr. Steinbeck (4)
The Bad Lands seemed like the work of an evil ____ (5)
The boat was named for Steinbeck's (4)
The east-west middle of the country was in ___, ND (5)
The poodle; companion to Mr. Steinbeck (7)
The truck (9)
These homes were revolutionary (6)
These trees cause wonder & respect in man (7)
This country wouldn't let Charley in (6)
This river, according to Mr. Steinbeck, should have been the east-west middle of the country (8)
Topic of family arguments (8)
Two cans of dog food were left for them (7)
White Mountains are in this state (5)
Wisconsin ___; formed by ice during the Ice Age (5)
You don't take one, one takes you (4)
____ With Charley (7)

Travels With Charley Word Search 2 Answer Key

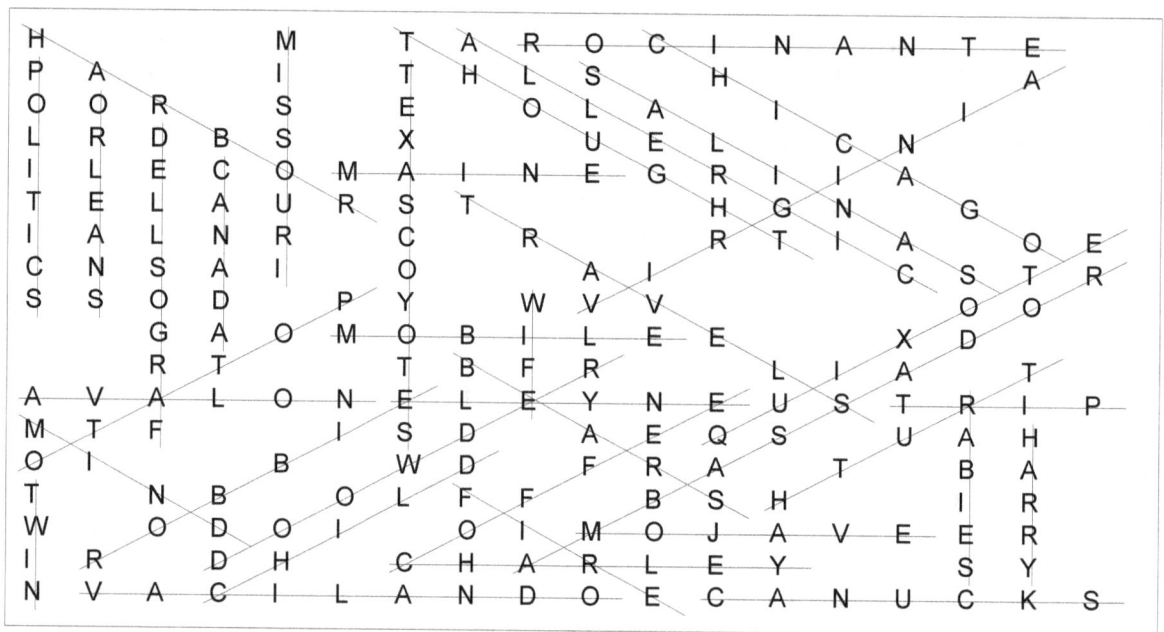

A man has to have feelings and then words before he can come close to this (7)
Charley didn't have his certificate of vaccination for this (6)
Charley wanted to fight them at Yellowstone (5)
Charley was ___ to insecticides (8)
Deer Isle was like ____ (6)
Desert Mr. Steinbeck and Charley crossed (6)
Fair ___; the boat (6)
Going somewhere with a direction in mind but not caring if you get there or not (9)
He wanted to be a hairdresser (6)
Hotel in Chicago: ___ East (10)
In this state Mr. Steinbeck realized his trip had ended (8)
It is the great get-together symbol (6)
Kind of sermon in Vermont: ___ & Brimstone (4)
Lonesome ___; previous occupant of the hotel room (5)
Maine's migrant farmers (7)
Minneapolis & St. Paul are the ___ Cities (4)
Mr. Steinbeck wanted to see these crops in Maine (6)
Mr. Steinbeck's home town in California (7)
Near the end of the book, Mr. Steinbeck gave reasons why he couldn't find the ___ about the country
New ___; place where the Cheerleaders demonstrated (7)
Only state to enter the union by treaty (5)
Place where Mr. Steinbeck's wife met him to visit (7)
Rocinante was named for Don ___'s horse (7)
Sag ___; starting point of the trip (6)
Texas is a state of ____, according to Mr. Steinbeck (4)
The Bad Lands seemed like the work of an evil ____ (5)
The boat was named for Steinbeck's (4)
The east-west middle of the country was in ___, ND (5)
The poodle; companion to Mr. Steinbeck (7)
The truck (9)
These homes were revolutionary (6)
These trees cause wonder & respect in man (7)
This country wouldn't let Charley in (6)
This river, according to Mr. Steinbeck, should have been the east-west middle of the country (8)
Topic of family arguments (8)
Two cans of dog food were left for them (7)
White Mountains are in this state (5)
Wisconsin ___; formed by ice during the Ice Age (5)
You don't take one, one takes you (4)
____ With Charley (7)

Travels With Charley Word Search 3

```
M O N T A N A I F A R G O M N B Y K
Z O B O T P V C L B A V C A I M H L
T Z J T G S A E T E B I O I W N F P
S W N A L P C B S A I R Y N T M D W
R R J T V P I R T R E G O E R I F K
E O P O S E L E E S S I T L E S S K
I D B P G J A A I R T N E E D S C J
C A C B G F N K N O H I S Y W O I D
A S C H I L D E B C O A X N O U T N
L S B X A E O R E I U R T E O R I H
G A J D T R P T C N G N L T D I L J
A B W S M D L W K A H F E E F F O C
V M V X O E K E X N T C T W A M P K
A A X T B L G V Y T M X H R I N Y J
L S A N I L A S T E X A S I U F S K
O G Q J L S K C U N A C K M C T E Z
N Y B S E H A R R Y T R O B R A H X
C A N A D A F T R A V E L S S J G Z
A L L E R G I C C Q U I X O T E M O
K P G R C H E E R L E A D E R S J F
```

ALLERGIC	FIRE	RABIES
AMBASSADOR	GLACIERS	REDWOOD
AVALON	HARBOR	ROBBIE
BEARS	HARRY	ROCINANTE
CANADA	ICEBREAKER	SALINAS
CANUCKS	MAINE	STEINBECK
CHARLEY	MIND	TEXAS
CHEERLEADERS	MISSOURI	THOUGHT
CHICAGO	MOBILE	TRAVELS
CHILD	MOJAVE	TRIP
COFFEE	MONTANA	TRUTH
COYOTES	ORLEANS	TWIN
DELLS	POLITICS	VACILANDO
ELEYNE	POTATO	VIRGINIA
FARGO	QUIXOTE	WIFE

Travels With Charley Word Search 3 Answer Key

M	O	N	T	A	N	A	I	F	A	R	G	O	M	N										
	O		J	O		V	C		B	A	V		C	I	W									
			A	T		A	E	S	E	B	I	R	O	N	N	M		D						
S		R	T	A	V	C	B	T	A	I	R	O	Y	E	T	I	F							
R	O		A	O	P	I	R	E	R	E	G	T	O	L	R	S	S							
E	D	B	P	P	E	L	E	I	S	N	I	H	T	E	E	S	C							
I	A	C	B			A	K	N	R	B	N	O	E	Y	D	O	I							
C	S	C	H	I	L	D	E	B	O	E	I	U	S	N	W	U	T							
A	S			A	R	E	R	E	C	C	A	R		E	O	R	I							
L				M	D	L	K	C	I	N	H		L	E	O	I	L							
G	A	B		O	E			K	N	T	R		E	F	F	O	P							
A	M			B	L	E		Y	A	C	T	H	W	A	I	N								C
V	A	S	A	N	I	L	A	S	T	E	X	A	S	R	U	F	S	H						
L					L	S	K	C	U	N	A	C		I	U	E	G							
O					E	H	A	R	R	Y	O	B	R	A										
N				A	N	A	D	A	T	R	A	V	E	L	S									
C	A	L	L	E	R	G	I	C	Q	U	I	X	O	T	E	O								
					C	H	E	E	R	L	E	A	D	E	R	S								

ALLERGIC
AMBASSADOR
AVALON
BEARS
CANADA
CANUCKS
CHARLEY
CHEERLEADERS
CHICAGO
CHILD
COFFEE
COYOTES
DELLS
ELEYNE
FARGO
FIRE
GLACIERS
HARBOR
HARRY
ICEBREAKER
MAINE
MIND
MISSOURI
MOBILE
MOJAVE
MONTANA
ORLEANS
POLITICS
POTATO
QUIXOTE
RABIES
REDWOOD
ROBBIE
ROCINANTE
SALINAS
STEINBECK
TEXAS
THOUGHT
TRAVELS
TRIP
TRUTH
TWIN
VACILANDO
VIRGINIA
WIFE

Travels With Charley Word Search 4

```
O V I R G I N I A S F H A R R Y X Q
D C H I C A G O R S M A I N E R S J G
N C D T D M B E S G N H K S O E S F
A C N A X H I L H F S A T G B I C S
L F N M R C L M A X E W T C B B R O
I A E T A E X M R R I R Y T I A G Q
C H I L D K C E B N I E T S E R I F
A H G R E L F E O P F L H B A X V X
V T A Q K Y C J R I L I O F C C A B
S Q R R J I N O W L D B U T O H R S
C A U A L G C E R N S O G I Y E E Y
V O L I V E D A I L T M H R O E D Y
P T F I X E Y M N Z E S T U T R W R
O R M F N O L Z S U J A N O E L O K
L U O Y E A T S Y F C C N S S E O F
I T J P C E S E Y Y V K B S L A D G
T H A M O N T A N A V T S I D D Q K
I Y V A M B A S S A D O R M D E F H
C H E A V A L O N T R U C K E R S S
S A L L E R G I C P O T A T O S H G
```

ALLERGIC
AMBASSADOR
AVALON
BEARS
CANADA
CANUCKS
CHARLEY
CHEERLEADERS
CHICAGO
CHILD
COFFEE
COYOTES
DELLS
ELEYNE
FARGO
FIRE
GLACIERS
HARBOR
HARRY
ICEBREAKER
MAINE
MIND
MISSOURI
MOBILE
MOJAVE
MONTANA
ORLEANS
POLITICS
POTATO
QUIXOTE
RABIES
REDWOOD
ROBBIE
SALINAS
STEINBECK
TEXAS
THOUGHT
TRAVELS
TRIP
TRUCKERS
TRUTH
TWIN
VACILANDO
VIRGINIA
WIFE

Travels With Charley Word Search 4 Answer Key

ALLERGIC	FIRE	RABIES
AMBASSADOR	GLACIERS	REDWOOD
AVALON	HARBOR	ROBBIE
BEARS	HARRY	SALINAS
CANADA	ICEBREAKER	STEINBECK
CANUCKS	MAINE	TEXAS
CHARLEY	MIND	THOUGHT
CHEERLEADERS	MISSOURI	TRAVELS
CHICAGO	MOBILE	TRIP
CHILD	MOJAVE	TRUCKERS
COFFEE	MONTANA	TRUTH
COYOTES	ORLEANS	TWIN
DELLS	POLITICS	VACILANDO
ELEYNE	POTATO	VIRGINIA
FARGO	QUIXOTE	WIFE

Travels With Charley Crossword 1

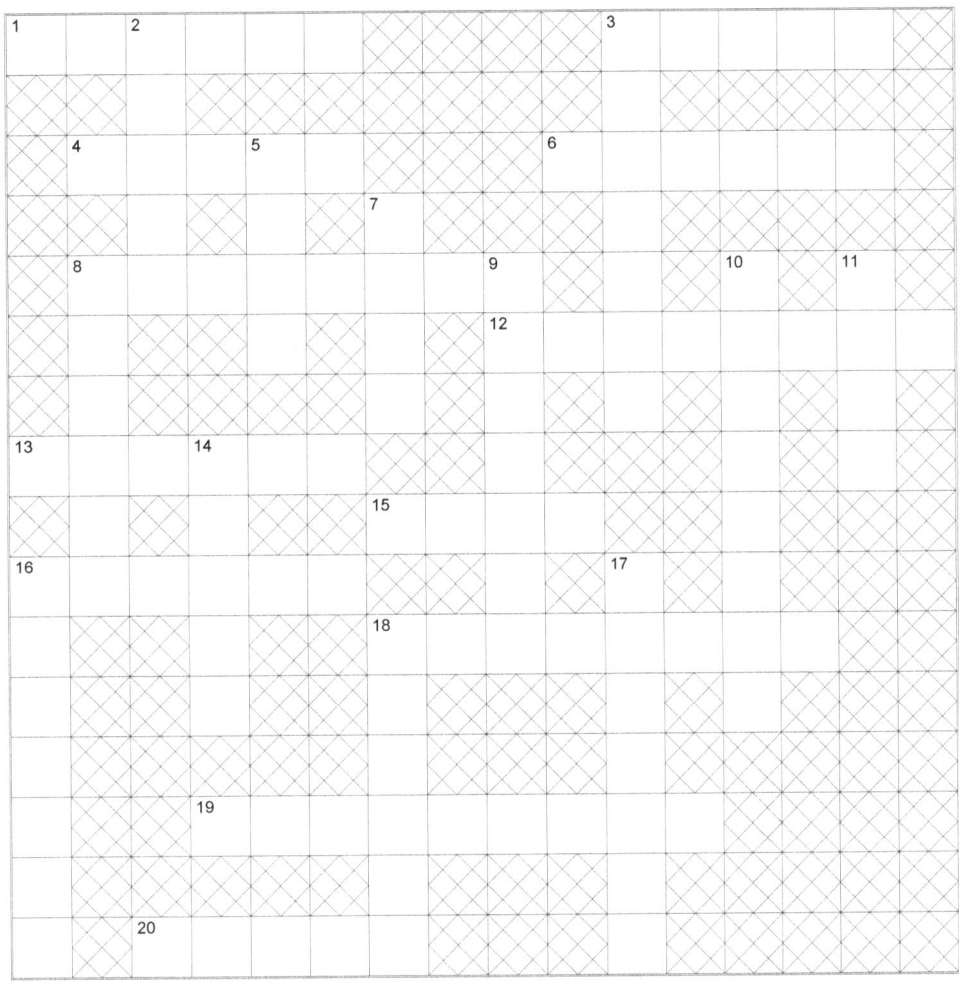

Across
1. It is the great get-together symbol
3. Only state to enter the union by treaty
4. Near the end of the book, Mr. Steinbeck gave reasons why he couldn't find the ___ about the country
6. Charley didn't have his certificate of vaccination for this
8. Topic of family arguments
12. Charley was ___ to insecticides
13. Sag ___; starting point of the trip
15. Texas is a state of ____, according to Mr. Steinbeck
16. Desert Mr. Steinbeck and Charley crossed
18. This river, according to Mr. Steinbeck, should have been the east-west middle of the country
19. The truck
20. White Mountains are in this state

Down
2. The east-west middle of the country was in ___, ND
3. ____ With Charley
5. Minneapolis & St. Paul are the ___ Cities
7. Kind of sermon in Vermont: ___ & Brimstone
8. Mr. Steinbeck wanted to see these crops in Maine
9. Mr. Steinbeck's home town in California
10. They have their own language, according to Mr. Steinbeck
11. The boat was named for Steinbeck's
14. Charley wanted to fight them at Yellowstone
16. State Mr. Steinbeck considered a great splash of grandeur
17. Two cans of dog food were left for them
18. These homes were revolutionary

Travels With Charley Crossword 1 Answer Key

	1 C	2 O	F	F	E	E				3 T	E	X	A	S
		F	A							R				
	4 T	R	U	5 T	H			6 R	A	B	I	E	S	
		G		W		7 F		V						
	8 P	O	L	I	T	I	C	9 S		10 T		11 W		
		O		N		R		12 A	L	L	E	R	G	I	C
		T				E		L		S		U		F	
13 H	A	R	14 B	O	R			I				C		E	
	T		E			15 M	I	N	D			K			
16 M	O	J	A	V	E			A		17 C		E			
O			R			18 M	I	S	S	O	U	R	I		
N			S			O				Y		S			
T						B				O					
A			19 R	O	C	I	N	A	N	T	E				
N						L				E					
A			20 M	A	I	N	E			S					

Across
1. It is the great get-together symbol
3. Only state to enter the union by treaty
4. Near the end of the book, Mr. Steinbeck gave reasons why he couldn't find the ___ about the country
6. Charley didn't have his certificate of vaccination for this
8. Topic of family arguments
12. Charley was ___ to insecticides
13. Sag ___; starting point of the trip
15. Texas is a state of ____, according to Mr. Steinbeck
16. Desert Mr. Steinbeck and Charley crossed
18. This river, according to Mr. Steinbeck, should have been the east-west middle of the country
19. The truck
20. White Mountains are in this state

Down
2. The east-west middle of the country was in ___, ND
3. ____ With Charley
5. Minneapolis & St. Paul are the ___ Cities
7. Kind of sermon in Vermont: ___ & Brimstone
8. Mr. Steinbeck wanted to see these crops in Maine
9. Mr. Steinbeck's home town in California
10. They have their own language, according to Mr. Steinbeck
11. The boat was named for Steinbeck's
14. Charley wanted to fight them at Yellowstone
16. State Mr. Steinbeck considered a great splash of grandeur
17. Two cans of dog food were left for them
18. These homes were revolutionary

Travels With Charley Crossword 2

Across
1. Minneapolis & St. Paul are the ___ Cities
2. Maine's migrant farmers
4. Charley didn't have his certificate of vaccination for this
5. Topic of family arguments
7. Charley was ___ to insecticides
9. The boat was named for Steinbeck's
10. Texas is a state of ____, according to Mr. Steinbeck
13. This river, according to Mr. Steinbeck, should have been the east-west middle of the country
15. The east-west middle of the country was in ___, ND
17. Wisconsin ___; formed by ice during the Ice Age
18. Deer Isle was like ____

Down
1. Near the end of the book, Mr. Steinbeck gave reasons why he couldn't find the ___ about the country
2. The poodle; companion to Mr. Steinbeck
3. Fair ___; the boat
5. Mr. Steinbeck wanted to see these crops in Maine
6. Mr. Steinbeck's home town in California
8. It is the great get-together symbol
11. Sag ___; starting point of the trip
12. State Mr. Steinbeck considered a great splash of grandeur
13. These homes were revolutionary
14. These trees cause wonder & respect in man
15. Kind of sermon in Vermont: ___ & Brimstone
16. Only state to enter the union by treaty

Travels With Charley Crossword 2 Answer Key

				1 T	W	I	N		2 C	A	N	U	C	K	S
				R					H						
		3 E		U				4 R	A	B	I	E	S		
5 P	O	L	I	T	I	C	S	6 S	R						
O		E		H				7 A	L	L	E	R	G	8 I	C
T		Y						L	E						O
A		N						I	Y			9 W	I	F	E
T		E				10 M	I	N	D					F	
O			11 H			A			12 M					E	
			A		13 M	I	S	S	O	U	R	14 I		E	
	15 F	A	R	G	O				N			E			
	I		B		B		16 T		T		17 D	E	L	L	S
	R		O		I		E		A		W				
	E		R		L		X		N		O				
					E		18 A	V	A	L	O	N			
							S				D				

Across
1. Minneapolis & St. Paul are the ___ Cities
2. Maine's migrant farmers
4. Charley didn't have his certificate of vaccination for this
5. Topic of family arguments
7. Charley was ___ to insecticides
9. The boat was named for Steinbeck's
10. Texas is a state of ____, according to Mr. Steinbeck
13. This river, according to Mr. Steinbeck, should have been the east-west middle of the country
15. The east-west middle of the country was in ___, ND
17. Wisconsin ___; formed by ice during the Ice Age
18. Deer Isle was like ____

Down
1. Near the end of the book, Mr. Steinbeck gave reasons why he couldn't find the ___ about the country
2. The poodle; companion to Mr. Steinbeck
3. Fair ___; the boat
5. Mr. Steinbeck wanted to see these crops in Maine
6. Mr. Steinbeck's home town in California
8. It is the great get-together symbol
11. Sag ___; starting point of the trip
12. State Mr. Steinbeck considered a great splash of grandeur
13. These homes were revolutionary
14. These trees cause wonder & respect in man
15. Kind of sermon in Vermont: ___ & Brimstone
16. Only state to enter the union by treaty

Travels With Charley Crossword 3

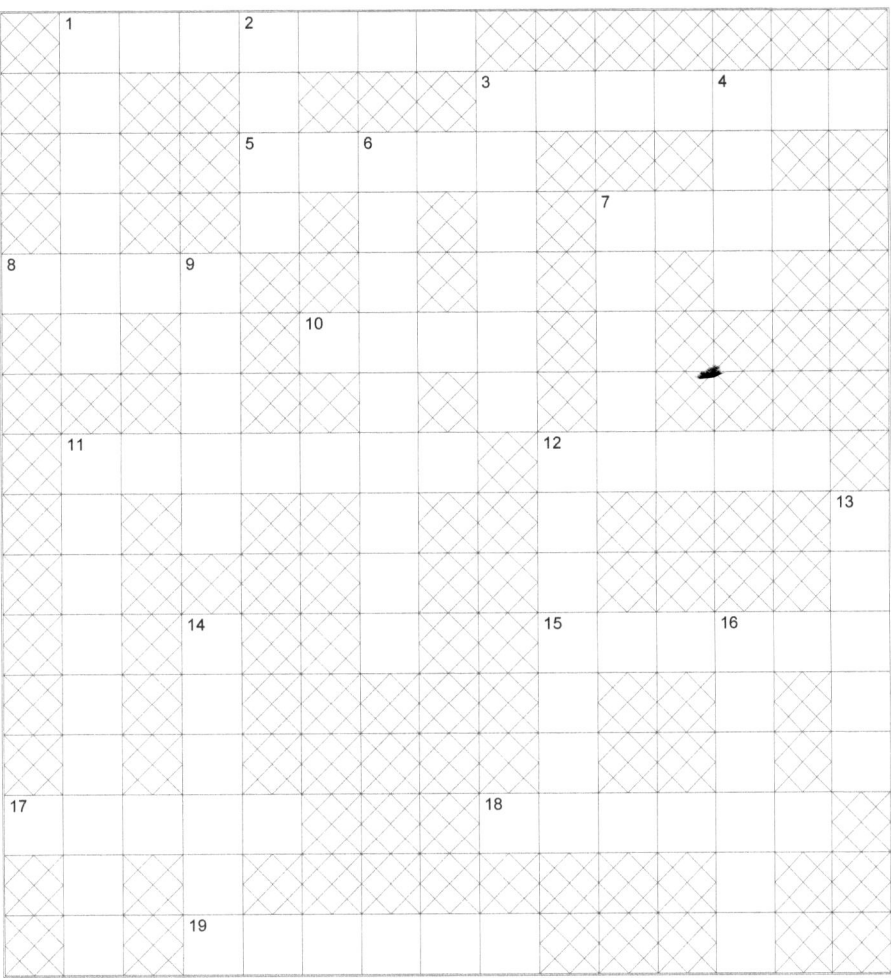

Across
1. These trees cause wonder & respect in man
3. Two cans of dog food were left for them
5. The east-west middle of the country was in ___, ND
7. You don't take one, one takes you
8. Texas is a state of ____, according to Mr. Steinbeck
10. Kind of sermon in Vermont: ___ & Brimstone
11. Mr. Steinbeck's home town in California
12. The Bad Lands seemed like the work of an evil ____
15. This country wouldn't let Charley in
17. Only state to enter the union by treaty
18. These homes were revolutionary
19. Fair ___; the boat

Down
1. He wanted to be a hairdresser
2. The boat was named for Steinbeck's
3. It is the great get-together symbol
4. Minneapolis & St. Paul are the ___ Cities
6. The truck
7. Near the end of the book, Mr. Steinbeck gave reasons why he couldn't find the ___ about the country
9. Wisconsin ___; formed by ice during the Ice Age
11. Author
12. Place where Mr. Steinbeck's wife met him to visit
13. Charley wanted to fight them at Yellowstone
14. Desert Mr. Steinbeck and Charley crossed
16. Deer Isle was like ____

Travels With Charley Crossword 3 Answer Key

	1 R	E	D	2 W	O	O	D				
	O			I				3 C	O	Y	O	T	E	S
	B		5 F	A	6 R	G	O				W
	B		E		O		F		7 T	R	I	P
8 M	I	9 N	D			C		F		R		N
	E		E		10 F	I	R	E		U
			L			N		E		T
	11 S	A	L	I	N	A	S		12 C	H	I	L	D
	T		S			N			H				13 B
	E					T			I				E
	I		14 M			E			15 C	A	N	16 A	D	A
	N		O						A			V		R
	B		J						G			A		S
17 T	E	X	A	S				18 M	O	B	I	L	E
	C		V									O
	K		19 E	L	E	Y	N	E				N

Across

1. These trees cause wonder & respect in man
3. Two cans of dog food were left for them
5. The east-west middle of the country was in ___, ND
7. You don't take one, one takes you
8. Texas is a state of ____, according to Mr. Steinbeck
10. Kind of sermon in Vermont: ___ & Brimstone
11. Mr. Steinbeck's home town in California
12. The Bad Lands seemed like the work of an evil ____
15. This country wouldn't let Charley in
17. Only state to enter the union by treaty
18. These homes were revolutionary
19. Fair ___; the boat

Down

1. He wanted to be a hairdresser
2. The boat was named for Steinbeck's
3. It is the great get-together symbol
4. Minneapolis & St. Paul are the ___ Cities
6. The truck
7. Near the end of the book, Mr. Steinbeck gave reasons why he couldn't find the ___ about the country
9. Wisconsin ___; formed by ice during the Ice Age
11. Author
12. Place where Mr. Steinbeck's wife met him to visit
13. Charley wanted to fight them at Yellowstone
14. Desert Mr. Steinbeck and Charley crossed
16. Deer Isle was like ____

Travels With Charley Crossword 4

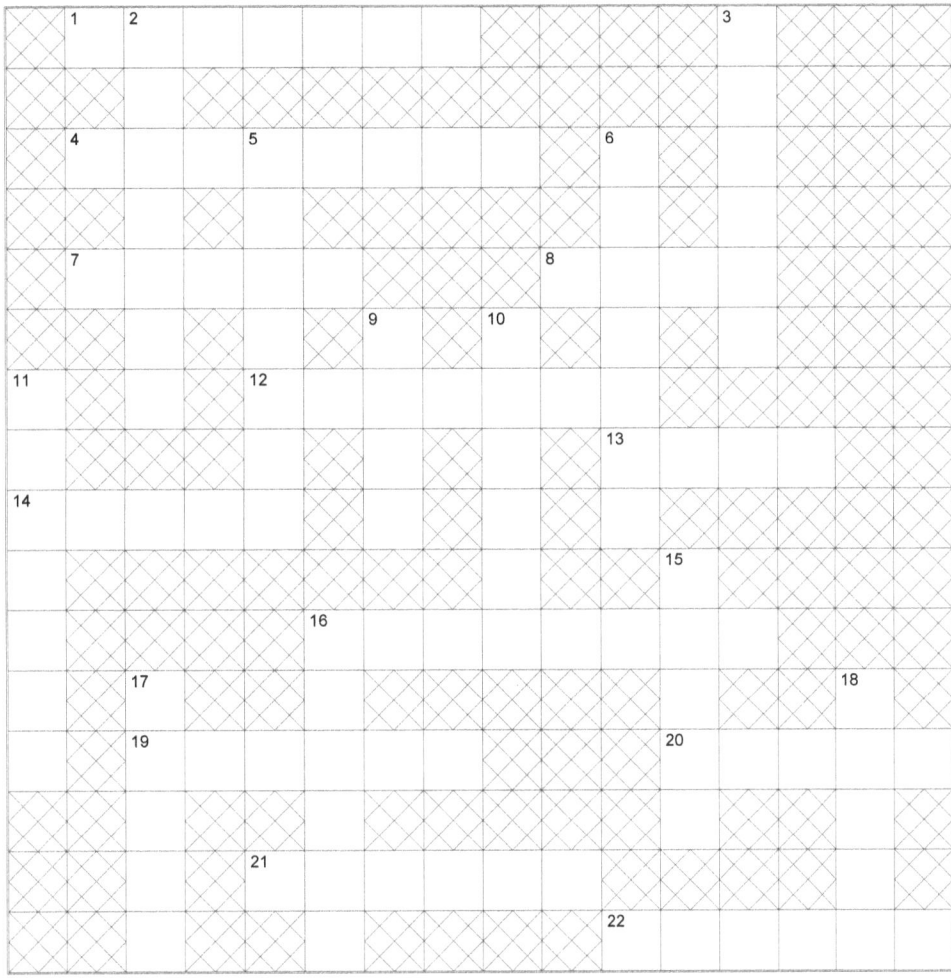

Across
1. State Mr. Steinbeck considered a great splash of grandeur
4. Responsible for wiping out most of the redwood trees
7. White Mountains are in this state
8. The boat was named for Steinbeck's
12. Place where Mr. Steinbeck's wife met him to visit
13. Minneapolis & St. Paul are the ___ Cities
14. Wisconsin ___; formed by ice during the Ice Age
16. This river, according to Mr. Steinbeck, should have been the east-west middle of the country
19. Sag ___; starting point of the trip
20. Only state to enter the union by treaty
21. Fair ___; the boat
22. Deer Isle was like ____

Down
2. New ___; place where the Cheerleaders demonstrated
3. It is the great get-together symbol
5. Maine's migrant farmers
6. Rocinante was named for Don ___'s horse
9. Kind of sermon in Vermont: ___ & Brimstone
10. Charley didn't have his certificate of vaccination for this
11. These trees cause wonder & respect in man
15. Near the end of the book, Mr. Steinbeck gave reasons why he couldn't find the ___ about the country
16. These homes were revolutionary
17. The Bad Lands seemed like the work of an evil ____
18. The east-west middle of the country was in ___, ND

Travels With Charley Crossword 4 Answer Key

	1 M	2 O	N	T	A	N	A			3 C		
		R								O		
	4 G	L	5 A	C	I	E	R	S	6 Q		F	
		E		A					U		F	
	7 M	A	I	N	E			8 W	I	F	E	
		N		U		9 F		10 R	X		E	
11 R		S		12 C	H	I	C	A	G	O		
E				K		R		B		13 T	W	I	N
14 D	E	L	L	S		E		I		E		
W								E		15 T		
O						16 M	I	S	S	O	U	R	I
O		17 C		O						U		18 F
19 D		H	A	R	B	O	R			20 T	E	X	A	S
		I			I					H		R
		21 L		E	L	E	Y	N	E			G
		D			E					22 A	V	A	L	O	N

Across

1. State Mr. Steinbeck considered a great splash of grandeur
4. Responsible for wiping out most of the redwood trees
7. White Mountains are in this state
8. The boat was named for Steinbeck's
12. Place where Mr. Steinbeck's wife met him to visit
13. Minneapolis & St. Paul are the ___ Cities
14. Wisconsin ___; formed by ice during the Ice Age
16. This river, according to Mr. Steinbeck, should have been the east-west middle of the country
19. Sag ___; starting point of the trip
20. Only state to enter the union by treaty
21. Fair ___; the boat
22. Deer Isle was like ____

Down

2. New ___; place where the Cheerleaders demonstrated
3. It is the great get-together symbol
5. Maine's migrant farmers
6. Rocinante was named for Don ___'s horse
9. Kind of sermon in Vermont: ___ & Brimstone
10. Charley didn't have his certificate of vaccination for this
11. These trees cause wonder & respect in man
15. Near the end of the book, Mr. Steinbeck gave reasons why he couldn't find the ___ about the country
16. These homes were revolutionary
17. The Bad Lands seemed like the work of an evil ____
18. The east-west middle of the country was in ___, ND

Travels With Charley

TRUTH	GLACIERS	TWIN	ORLEANS	ICEBREAKER
MOJAVE	ROCINANTE	AVALON	MOBILE	ELEYNE
HARRY	TEXAS	FREE SPACE	REDWOOD	THOUGHT
RABIES	CHILD	ROBBIE	CHARLEY	POTATO
CHEERLEADERS	CANADA	MIND	POLITICS	BEARS

Travels With Charley

CHICAGO	MISSOURI	MAINE	MONTANA	FIRE
QUIXOTE	WIFE	VACILANDO	TRAVELS	SALINAS
ALLERGIC	TRIP	FREE SPACE	TRUCKERS	FARGO
AMBASSADOR	HARBOR	STEINBECK	VIRGINIA	COYOTES
DELLS	BEARS	POLITICS	MIND	CANADA

Travels With Charley

HARRY	COFFEE	MOBILE	TRUTH	WIFE
BEARS	MAINE	STEINBECK	CHEERLEADERS	COYOTES
TRUCKERS	SALINAS	FREE SPACE	CHARLEY	AMBASSADOR
TRIP	ICEBREAKER	RABIES	MISSOURI	CHICAGO
ROBBIE	FARGO	TWIN	QUIXOTE	POLITICS

Travels With Charley

THOUGHT	DELLS	ORLEANS	ALLERGIC	REDWOOD
MONTANA	CANADA	MOJAVE	MIND	TRAVELS
TEXAS	POTATO	FREE SPACE	VIRGINIA	FIRE
AVALON	CANUCKS	ELEYNE	HARBOR	CHILD
ROCINANTE	POLITICS	QUIXOTE	TWIN	FARGO

Travels With Charley

AMBASSADOR	VACILANDO	ORLEANS	ELEYNE	FIRE
WIFE	CHILD	CHICAGO	ROCINANTE	REDWOOD
RABIES	COFFEE	FREE SPACE	TWIN	MOJAVE
HARRY	COYOTES	MISSOURI	ICEBREAKER	CHEERLEADERS
ROBBIE	THOUGHT	SALINAS	MOBILE	TRAVELS

Travels With Charley

TEXAS	TRIP	MONTANA	CHARLEY	FARGO
VIRGINIA	DELLS	QUIXOTE	MIND	POTATO
STEINBECK	TRUTH	FREE SPACE	CANUCKS	CANADA
BEARS	HARBOR	MAINE	AVALON	TRUCKERS
POLITICS	TRAVELS	MOBILE	SALINAS	THOUGHT

Travels With Charley

TRAVELS	CHICAGO	ALLERGIC	ELEYNE	GLACIERS
MAINE	RABIES	COFFEE	VIRGINIA	TRIP
AVALON	FARGO	FREE SPACE	TWIN	FIRE
CHARLEY	POTATO	TRUCKERS	ORLEANS	MOJAVE
BEARS	ROCINANTE	WIFE	COYOTES	MIND

Travels With Charley

QUIXOTE	THOUGHT	TEXAS	CHILD	CANADA
CHEERLEADERS	AMBASSADOR	STEINBECK	HARRY	POLITICS
SALINAS	ICEBREAKER	FREE SPACE	DELLS	REDWOOD
MISSOURI	TRUTH	VACILANDO	CANUCKS	MONTANA
MOBILE	MIND	COYOTES	WIFE	ROCINANTE

Travels With Charley

ORLEANS	MOBILE	SALINAS	COYOTES	ROCINANTE
TRUCKERS	MIND	MAINE	ICEBREAKER	FARGO
TEXAS	ELEYNE	FREE SPACE	ALLERGIC	QUIXOTE
BEARS	CHARLEY	CANADA	WIFE	TRAVELS
VACILANDO	MISSOURI	TWIN	AVALON	CHICAGO

Travels With Charley

CANUCKS	HARRY	RABIES	CHEERLEADERS	COFFEE
TRUTH	ROBBIE	AMBASSADOR	MOJAVE	CHILD
VIRGINIA	REDWOOD	FREE SPACE	FIRE	POTATO
THOUGHT	HARBOR	DELLS	MONTANA	POLITICS
GLACIERS	CHICAGO	AVALON	TWIN	MISSOURI

Travels With Charley

TRUCKERS	ORLEANS	MIND	MOJAVE	GLACIERS
CANUCKS	CHARLEY	TWIN	THOUGHT	AVALON
COYOTES	MISSOURI	FREE SPACE	BEARS	TEXAS
MOBILE	POLITICS	POTATO	HARBOR	FIRE
TRAVELS	ROBBIE	FARGO	WIFE	TRIP

Travels With Charley

VIRGINIA	MAINE	QUIXOTE	RABIES	CANADA
CHICAGO	CHILD	ELEYNE	REDWOOD	DELLS
COFFEE	MONTANA	FREE SPACE	AMBASSADOR	ALLERGIC
TRUTH	STEINBECK	VACILANDO	HARRY	SALINAS
CHEERLEADERS	TRIP	WIFE	FARGO	ROBBIE

Travels With Charley

MISSOURI	STEINBECK	CHEERLEADERS	ALLERGIC	ROBBIE
FIRE	TEXAS	POTATO	AVALON	VIRGINIA
TRUTH	CANADA	FREE SPACE	REDWOOD	WIFE
RABIES	BEARS	GLACIERS	COYOTES	MIND
TWIN	HARRY	ROCINANTE	FARGO	POLITICS

Travels With Charley

DELLS	CHARLEY	MOBILE	TRUCKERS	HARBOR
MAINE	QUIXOTE	CHILD	AMBASSADOR	MONTANA
ORLEANS	SALINAS	FREE SPACE	THOUGHT	TRIP
ELEYNE	VACILANDO	CANUCKS	MOJAVE	CHICAGO
ICEBREAKER	POLITICS	FARGO	ROCINANTE	HARRY

Travels With Charley

AVALON	CHEERLEADERS	CANUCKS	BEARS	RABIES
ELEYNE	QUIXOTE	POLITICS	CHILD	FIRE
ROCINANTE	REDWOOD	FREE SPACE	WIFE	TRUTH
VIRGINIA	MOJAVE	CHICAGO	AMBASSADOR	TRUCKERS
TWIN	ORLEANS	CHARLEY	MISSOURI	ROBBIE

Travels With Charley

ALLERGIC	HARBOR	TRAVELS	TRIP	HARRY
GLACIERS	TEXAS	POTATO	CANADA	MOBILE
DELLS	SALINAS	FREE SPACE	ICEBREAKER	COFFEE
COYOTES	STEINBECK	VACILANDO	MONTANA	FARGO
MAINE	ROBBIE	MISSOURI	CHARLEY	ORLEANS

Travels With Charley

MAINE	STEINBECK	FIRE	AVALON	DELLS
MISSOURI	ORLEANS	THOUGHT	FARGO	ROCINANTE
HARRY	TEXAS	FREE SPACE	MOBILE	CHARLEY
VIRGINIA	TRUCKERS	MIND	ALLERGIC	CANADA
VACILANDO	HARBOR	MOJAVE	COFFEE	QUIXOTE

Travels With Charley

BEARS	POTATO	ROBBIE	COYOTES	TRIP
TWIN	WIFE	GLACIERS	CHEERLEADERS	AMBASSADOR
SALINAS	CHILD	FREE SPACE	MONTANA	RABIES
ICEBREAKER	CANUCKS	ELEYNE	POLITICS	REDWOOD
TRAVELS	QUIXOTE	COFFEE	MOJAVE	HARBOR

Travels With Charley

COYOTES	MISSOURI	VIRGINIA	ROCINANTE	DELLS
GLACIERS	FIRE	TRAVELS	CHARLEY	ALLERGIC
COFFEE	FARGO	FREE SPACE	TRUCKERS	THOUGHT
HARRY	RABIES	AMBASSADOR	POTATO	MIND
TRIP	ROBBIE	CHILD	WIFE	CANUCKS

Travels With Charley

TEXAS	ORLEANS	ELEYNE	MOBILE	SALINAS
BEARS	TWIN	POLITICS	STEINBECK	AVALON
ICEBREAKER	CANADA	FREE SPACE	QUIXOTE	HARBOR
TRUTH	MAINE	CHEERLEADERS	REDWOOD	CHICAGO
VACILANDO	CANUCKS	WIFE	CHILD	ROBBIE

Travels With Charley

MAINE	AMBASSADOR	MOJAVE	HARBOR	THOUGHT
FARGO	MONTANA	HARRY	ORLEANS	STEINBECK
CHICAGO	REDWOOD	FREE SPACE	TRUCKERS	GLACIERS
ICEBREAKER	MOBILE	VIRGINIA	BEARS	POTATO
CANADA	QUIXOTE	SALINAS	TRUTH	TRIP

Travels With Charley

AVALON	MIND	TEXAS	ROCINANTE	TWIN
DELLS	COYOTES	CHEERLEADERS	RABIES	ELEYNE
VACILANDO	ALLERGIC	FREE SPACE	MISSOURI	CHARLEY
POLITICS	COFFEE	ROBBIE	CANUCKS	WIFE
TRAVELS	TRIP	TRUTH	SALINAS	QUIXOTE

Travels With Charley

MOJAVE	MIND	VACILANDO	TRAVELS	POLITICS
TEXAS	QUIXOTE	TWIN	CANADA	HARBOR
FARGO	HARRY	FREE SPACE	SALINAS	FIRE
CANUCKS	WIFE	REDWOOD	CHILD	MONTANA
ALLERGIC	ELEYNE	AVALON	TRUTH	CHARLEY

Travels With Charley

CHICAGO	TRUCKERS	ICEBREAKER	STEINBECK	MISSOURI
ROBBIE	THOUGHT	ROCINANTE	MOBILE	DELLS
COYOTES	TRIP	FREE SPACE	BEARS	VIRGINIA
COFFEE	RABIES	GLACIERS	MAINE	CHEERLEADERS
POTATO	CHARLEY	TRUTH	AVALON	ELEYNE

Travels With Charley

DELLS	MAINE	HARRY	ROCINANTE	CHICAGO
CHARLEY	TRIP	REDWOOD	CHEERLEADERS	AVALON
COYOTES	ORLEANS	FREE SPACE	AMBASSADOR	POTATO
HARBOR	TWIN	FIRE	ELEYNE	MIND
FARGO	ALLERGIC	MISSOURI	CANADA	ICEBREAKER

Travels With Charley

SALINAS	GLACIERS	TRAVELS	TRUCKERS	BEARS
CHILD	STEINBECK	ROBBIE	POLITICS	QUIXOTE
MOBILE	TRUTH	FREE SPACE	WIFE	TEXAS
THOUGHT	CANUCKS	MONTANA	VIRGINIA	MOJAVE
RABIES	ICEBREAKER	CANADA	MISSOURI	ALLERGIC

Travels With Charley

TRAVELS	ROCINANTE	THOUGHT	TEXAS	COYOTES
AVALON	CHICAGO	MAINE	MISSOURI	POLITICS
ROBBIE	WIFE	FREE SPACE	VIRGINIA	CHILD
POTATO	HARRY	TRIP	MOBILE	REDWOOD
GLACIERS	CANADA	ALLERGIC	TRUTH	COFFEE

Travels With Charley

MONTANA	VACILANDO	MIND	FARGO	SALINAS
CHEERLEADERS	ICEBREAKER	FIRE	DELLS	QUIXOTE
ELEYNE	CHARLEY	FREE SPACE	HARBOR	CANUCKS
MOJAVE	RABIES	BEARS	ORLEANS	AMBASSADOR
TWIN	COFFEE	TRUTH	ALLERGIC	CANADA

Travels With Charley

MISSOURI	ROBBIE	ORLEANS	FIRE	MIND
POLITICS	MOJAVE	DELLS	WIFE	THOUGHT
TRAVELS	COFFEE	FREE SPACE	ALLERGIC	FARGO
TRUCKERS	COYOTES	SALINAS	STEINBECK	QUIXOTE
ELEYNE	TEXAS	VACILANDO	MONTANA	TWIN

Travels With Charley

CANADA	HARRY	VIRGINIA	CHARLEY	TRIP
TRUTH	ICEBREAKER	HARBOR	BEARS	RABIES
AMBASSADOR	MAINE	FREE SPACE	CHEERLEADERS	CHILD
MOBILE	AVALON	POTATO	GLACIERS	CHICAGO
ROCINANTE	TWIN	MONTANA	VACILANDO	TEXAS

Travels With Charley

COYOTES	MAINE	HARBOR	AVALON	ELEYNE
ROBBIE	BEARS	CHICAGO	VIRGINIA	FARGO
ORLEANS	TRUTH	FREE SPACE	CANUCKS	MOJAVE
HARRY	QUIXOTE	RABIES	CHILD	DELLS
SALINAS	COFFEE	POTATO	VACILANDO	CHARLEY

Travels With Charley

ICEBREAKER	TEXAS	TWIN	POLITICS	MISSOURI
FIRE	MIND	STEINBECK	ALLERGIC	AMBASSADOR
THOUGHT	CANADA	FREE SPACE	MONTANA	TRIP
MOBILE	TRUCKERS	GLACIERS	TRAVELS	REDWOOD
ROCINANTE	CHARLEY	VACILANDO	POTATO	COFFEE

Travels With Charley Vocabulary Word List

No.	Word	Clue/Definition
1.	AESTHETIC	Pertaining to the sense of beauty
2.	ANARCHISM	Theory that all governments are bad & should be abolished
3.	ANTIDOTE	Anything that relieves or counteracts an injurious effect
4.	APEX	Highest point; culmination
5.	APHIDS	Small soft-bodied insects that suck sap from plants
6.	APLOMB	Poise; self-confidence; assurance
7.	ATROPHIED	Wasted away
8.	AVID	Eager
9.	CALLOW	Immature; inexperienced
10.	CLOISTERED	Sheltered
11.	COERCION	Forcing to think or act in a certain manner by threat or force
12.	CONCISE	Expressing much in a few words
13.	CONDUCIVE	Helping to bring about an event
14.	CONSUMMATE	Skilled; perfect
15.	CORPULENCE	Being fat
16.	CORROBORATE	Attested to the truth or accuracy of something
17.	COURTEOUS	Polite
18.	CUR	Inferior or undesirable dog
19.	DAWDLE	Wasting time lingering
20.	DEBRIS	Scattered remains of something broken
21.	DECADENT	Condition or process of moral decay
22.	DEPLORE	Lament; feel or express deep sorrow
23.	DISPEL	To rid of by or as if by driving away or scattering
24.	DOCILE	Teachable; yielding; able to be formed
25.	ELATE	Raise the spirits of; make joyful
26.	ENVOY	Messenger
27.	FRACAS	Noisy quarrel; brawl
28.	GALL	Nerve; impudence
29.	GOADED	Urged; prodded
30.	INALIENABLE	Absolute; not to be given up
31.	INCISED	Cut into
32.	INCORRIGIBLE	Can't be corrected or reformed
33.	INEPT	Clumsy; incompetent
34.	INVECTIVES	Abusive, insulting expressions
35.	KIN	Relatives
36.	LACONIC	Terse; concise; succinct
37.	MEDIOCRE	Neither good or bad; average; ordinary
38.	MISANTHROPY	Hatred of mankind
39.	NUISANCE	A source of inconvenience or bother
40.	OBLIQUE	Indirect or evasive in meaning or expression; not straightforward
41.	OBSEQUIOUS	Full of servile compliance; fawning
42.	OBSOLESCENCE	Being replaced by something newer
43.	OGRE	Anyone especially cruel, brutish, or hideous
44.	ORGY	A revel involving unrestrained indulgence
45.	OSTENTATION	Showiness to impress others
46.	PANDEMONIUM	Uproar & noise
47.	PARADOX	Seemingly contradictory statement that may nonetheless be true
48.	PERIPATETIC	Roaming; wandering
49.	PERNICIOUS	Destructive; harmful

Travels With Charley Vocabulary Word List Continued

No.	Word	Clue/Definition
50.	PISCINE	Relating to fish
51.	POSTULATE	Statement generally accepted without proof
52.	PRECIOUS	Valuable
53.	PREMISE	Statement on which an argument is based or from which a conclusion is drawn
54.	QUALMS	Bad or uneasy feeling
55.	SEMANTIC	Relating to language
56.	SIEGE	Attack
57.	SUBTLETIES	Details; refinements
58.	TACITURN	Not talkative
59.	TAWDRY	Gaudy & cheap
60.	TRAVAIL	Labor
61.	UBIQUITOUS	Seeming to be everywhere at one time
62.	VAGUELY	Not clearly expressed or defined
63.	VICARIOUS	Experienced through imaginative participation in the experiences of others
64.	VINTAGE	Classic; characterized by enduring appeal
65.	VITALITY	Energy; liveliness
66.	WREST	To obtain forcefully
67.	ZENITH	Upper region of the sky

Travels With Charley Vocabulary Fill In The Blanks 1

_____ 1. Scattered remains of something broken

_____ 2. Relatives

_____ 3. Uproar & noise

_____ 4. Neither good or bad; average; ordinary

_____ 5. Wasting time lingering

_____ 6. Details; refinements

_____ 7. Teachable; yielding; able to be formed

_____ 8. Immature; inexperienced

_____ 9. Expressing much in a few words

_____ 10. Experienced through imaginative participation in the experiences of others

_____ 11. Inferior or undesirable dog

_____ 12. Eager

_____ 13. Not clearly expressed or defined

_____ 14. Valuable

_____ 15. Theory that all governments are bad & should be abolished

_____ 16. Poise; self-confidence; assurance

_____ 17. Indirect or evasive in meaning or expression; not straightforward

_____ 18. Energy; liveliness

_____ 19. Anyone especially cruel, brutish, or hideous

_____ 20. Wasted away

Travels With Charley Vocabulary Fill In The Blanks 1 Answer Key

DEBRIS	1. Scattered remains of something broken
KIN	2. Relatives
PANDEMONIUM	3. Uproar & noise
MEDIOCRE	4. Neither good or bad; average; ordinary
DAWDLE	5. Wasting time lingering
SUBTLETIES	6. Details; refinements
DOCILE	7. Teachable; yielding; able to be formed
CALLOW	8. Immature; inexperienced
CONCISE	9. Expressing much in a few words
VICARIOUS	10. Experienced through imaginative participation in the experiences of others
CUR	11. Inferior or undesirable dog
AVID	12. Eager
VAGUELY	13. Not clearly expressed or defined
PRECIOUS	14. Valuable
ANARCHISM	15. Theory that all governments are bad & should be abolished
APLOMB	16. Poise; self-confidence; assurance
OBLIQUE	17. Indirect or evasive in meaning or expression; not straightforward
VITALITY	18. Energy; liveliness
OGRE	19. Anyone especially cruel, brutish, or hideous
ATROPHIED	20. Wasted away

Travels With Charley Vocabulary Fill In The Blanks 2

1. To rid of by or as if by driving away or scattering
2. Attack
3. Noisy quarrel; brawl
4. Statement on which an argument is based or from which a conclusion is drawn
5. Poise; self-confidence; assurance
6. A revel involving unrestrained indulgence
7. Relatives
8. Gaudy & cheap
9. Seemingly contradictory statement that may nonetheless be true
10. Helping to bring about an event
11. Skilled; perfect
12. Can't be corrected or reformed
13. Scattered remains of something broken
14. Roaming; wandering
15. Cut into
16. Theory that all governments are bad & should be abolished
17. Relating to language
18. Nerve; impudence
19. Messenger
20. Valuable

Travels With Charley Vocabulary Fill In The Blanks 2 Answer Key

DISPEL	1. To rid of by or as if by driving away or scattering
SIEGE	2. Attack
FRACAS	3. Noisy quarrel; brawl
PREMISE	4. Statement on which an argument is based or from which a conclusion is drawn
APLOMB	5. Poise; self-confidence; assurance
ORGY	6. A revel involving unrestrained indulgence
KIN	7. Relatives
TAWDRY	8. Gaudy & cheap
PARADOX	9. Seemingly contradictory statement that may nonetheless be true
CONDUCIVE	10. Helping to bring about an event
CONSUMMATE	11. Skilled; perfect
INCORRIGIBLE	12. Can't be corrected or reformed
DEBRIS	13. Scattered remains of something broken
PERIPATETIC	14. Roaming; wandering
INCISED	15. Cut into
ANARCHISM	16. Theory that all governments are bad & should be abolished
SEMANTIC	17. Relating to language
GALL	18. Nerve; impudence
ENVOY	19. Messenger
PRECIOUS	20. Valuable

Travels With Charley Vocabulary Fill In The Blanks 3

1. Relating to language
2. Urged; prodded
3. Being fat
4. Teachable; yielding; able to be formed
5. Polite
6. Full of servile compliance; fawning
7. Energy; liveliness
8. To rid of by or as if by driving away or scattering
9. Expressing much in a few words
10. Terse; concise; succinct
11. Bad or uneasy feeling
12. Relating to fish
13. Attested to the truth or accuracy of something
14. Highest point; culmination
15. Showiness to impress others
16. To obtain forcefully
17. Hatred of mankind
18. Wasted away
19. Statement on which an argument is based or from which a conclusion is drawn
20. Poise; self-confidence; assurance

Travels With Charley Vocabulary Fill In The Blanks 3 Answer Key

SEMANTIC	1. Relating to language
GOADED	2. Urged; prodded
CORPULENCE	3. Being fat
DOCILE	4. Teachable; yielding; able to be formed
COURTEOUS	5. Polite
OBSEQUIOUS	6. Full of servile compliance; fawning
VITALITY	7. Energy; liveliness
DISPEL	8. To rid of by or as if by driving away or scattering
CONCISE	9. Expressing much in a few words
LACONIC	10. Terse; concise; succinct
QUALMS	11. Bad or uneasy feeling
PISCINE	12. Relating to fish
CORROBORATE	13. Attested to the truth or accuracy of something
APEX	14. Highest point; culmination
OSTENTATION	15. Showiness to impress others
WREST	16. To obtain forcefully
MISANTHROPY	17. Hatred of mankind
ATROPHIED	18. Wasted away
PREMISE	19. Statement on which an argument is based or from which a conclusion is drawn
APLOMB	20. Poise; self-confidence; assurance

Travels With Charley Vocabulary Fill In The Blanks 4

1. Anyone especially cruel, brutish, or hideous
2. Immature; inexperienced
3. Not talkative
4. Upper region of the sky
5. Clumsy; incompetent
6. Attack
7. Teachable; yielding; able to be formed
8. Classic; characterized by enduring appeal
9. Raise the spirits of; make joyful
10. Helping to bring about an event
11. Lament; feel or express deep sorrow
12. To obtain forcefully
13. Neither good or bad; average; ordinary
14. Roaming; wandering
15. Theory that all governments are bad & should be abolished
16. Details; refinements
17. Sheltered
18. Attested to the truth or accuracy of something
19. Showiness to impress others
20. Full of servile compliance; fawning

Travels With Charley Vocabulary Fill In The Blanks 4 Answer Key

OGRE	1. Anyone especially cruel, brutish, or hideous
CALLOW	2. Immature; inexperienced
TACITURN	3. Not talkative
ZENITH	4. Upper region of the sky
INEPT	5. Clumsy; incompetent
SIEGE	6. Attack
DOCILE	7. Teachable; yielding; able to be formed
VINTAGE	8. Classic; characterized by enduring appeal
ELATE	9. Raise the spirits of; make joyful
CONDUCIVE	10. Helping to bring about an event
DEPLORE	11. Lament; feel or express deep sorrow
WREST	12. To obtain forcefully
MEDIOCRE	13. Neither good or bad; average; ordinary
PERIPATETIC	14. Roaming; wandering
ANARCHISM	15. Theory that all governments are bad & should be abolished
SUBTLETIES	16. Details; refinements
CLOISTERED	17. Sheltered
CORROBORATE	18. Attested to the truth or accuracy of something
OSTENTATION	19. Showiness to impress others
OBSEQUIOUS	20. Full of servile compliance; fawning

Travels With Charley Vocabulary Matching 1

___ 1. COURTEOUS   A. Can't be corrected or reformed
___ 2. QUALMS   B. Labor
___ 3. OBLIQUE   C. To rid of by or as if by driving away or scattering
___ 4. MISANTHROPY   D. Skilled; perfect
___ 5. MEDIOCRE   E. Statement generally accepted without proof
___ 6. DEPLORE   F. Indirect or evasive in meaning or expression; not straightforward
___ 7. CORPULENCE   G. Gaudy & cheap
___ 8. CONSUMMATE   H. To obtain forcefully
___ 9. INCORRIGIBLE   I. Valuable
___10. AESTHETIC   J. Roaming; wandering
___11. TAWDRY   K. Lament; feel or express deep sorrow
___12. ELATE   L. Being fat
___13. POSTULATE   M. Raise the spirits of; make joyful
___14. PRECIOUS   N. Details; refinements
___15. DISPEL   O. Nerve; impudence
___16. WREST   P. Pertaining to the sense of beauty
___17. DECADENT   Q. Polite
___18. SUBTLETIES   R. Attested to the truth or accuracy of something
___19. INALIENABLE   S. Neither good or bad; average; ordinary
___20. TRAVAIL   T. Hatred of mankind
___21. SIEGE   U. Attack
___22. GALL   V. Condition or process of moral decay
___23. PERIPATETIC   W. Bad or uneasy feeling
___24. ENVOY   X. Messenger
___25. CORROBORATE   Y. Absolute; not to be given up

Travels With Charley Vocabulary Matching 1 Answer Key

Q - 1. COURTEOUS	A.	Can't be corrected or reformed
W - 2. QUALMS	B.	Labor
F - 3. OBLIQUE	C.	To rid of by or as if by driving away or scattering
T - 4. MISANTHROPY	D.	Skilled; perfect
S - 5. MEDIOCRE	E.	Statement generally accepted without proof
K - 6. DEPLORE	F.	Indirect or evasive in meaning or expression; not straightforward
L - 7. CORPULENCE	G.	Gaudy & cheap
D - 8. CONSUMMATE	H.	To obtain forcefully
A - 9. INCORRIGIBLE	I.	Valuable
P - 10. AESTHETIC	J.	Roaming; wandering
G - 11. TAWDRY	K.	Lament; feel or express deep sorrow
M - 12. ELATE	L.	Being fat
E - 13. POSTULATE	M.	Raise the spirits of; make joyful
I - 14. PRECIOUS	N.	Details; refinements
C - 15. DISPEL	O.	Nerve; impudence
H - 16. WREST	P.	Pertaining to the sense of beauty
V - 17. DECADENT	Q.	Polite
N - 18. SUBTLETIES	R.	Attested to the truth or accuracy of something
Y - 19. INALIENABLE	S.	Neither good or bad; average; ordinary
B - 20. TRAVAIL	T.	Hatred of mankind
U - 21. SIEGE	U.	Attack
O - 22. GALL	V.	Condition or process of moral decay
J - 23. PERIPATETIC	W.	Bad or uneasy feeling
X - 24. ENVOY	X.	Messenger
R - 25. CORROBORATE	Y.	Absolute; not to be given up

Travels With Charley Vocabulary Matching 2

___ 1. INEPT
___ 2. GOADED
___ 3. CONDUCIVE
___ 4. INVECTIVES
___ 5. INCISED
___ 6. AESTHETIC
___ 7. ANARCHISM
___ 8. CLOISTERED
___ 9. QUALMS
___ 10. CUR
___ 11. DEPLORE
___ 12. TAWDRY
___ 13. WREST
___ 14. OBSEQUIOUS
___ 15. COURTEOUS
___ 16. PRECIOUS
___ 17. ENVOY
___ 18. NUISANCE
___ 19. ZENITH
___ 20. DEBRIS
___ 21. OGRE
___ 22. INCORRIGIBLE
___ 23. APEX
___ 24. VINTAGE
___ 25. CONCISE

A. Valuable
B. Messenger
C. Upper region of the sky
D. Anyone especially cruel, brutish, or hideous
E. Cut into
F. Pertaining to the sense of beauty
G. Classic; characterized by enduring appeal
H. Theory that all governments are bad & should be abolished
I. Abusive, insulting expressions
J. Highest point; culmination
K. To obtain forcefully
L. Expressing much in a few words
M. A source of inconvenience or bother
N. Sheltered
O. Helping to bring about an event
P. Can't be corrected or reformed
Q. Gaudy & cheap
R. Clumsy; incompetent
S. Polite
T. Full of servile compliance; fawning
U. Urged; prodded
V. Scattered remains of something broken
W. Bad or uneasy feeling
X. Inferior or undesirable dog
Y. Lament; feel or express deep sorrow

Travels With Charley Vocabulary Matching 2 Answer Key

R - 1. INEPT	A.	Valuable
U - 2. GOADED	B.	Messenger
O - 3. CONDUCIVE	C.	Upper region of the sky
I - 4. INVECTIVES	D.	Anyone especially cruel, brutish, or hideous
E - 5. INCISED	E.	Cut into
F - 6. AESTHETIC	F.	Pertaining to the sense of beauty
H - 7. ANARCHISM	G.	Classic; characterized by enduring appeal
N - 8. CLOISTERED	H.	Theory that all governments are bad & should be abolished
W - 9. QUALMS	I.	Abusive, insulting expressions
X - 10. CUR	J.	Highest point; culmination
Y - 11. DEPLORE	K.	To obtain forcefully
Q - 12. TAWDRY	L.	Expressing much in a few words
K - 13. WREST	M.	A source of inconvenience or bother
T - 14. OBSEQUIOUS	N.	Sheltered
S - 15. COURTEOUS	O.	Helping to bring about an event
A - 16. PRECIOUS	P.	Can't be corrected or reformed
B - 17. ENVOY	Q.	Gaudy & cheap
M - 18. NUISANCE	R.	Clumsy; incompetent
C - 19. ZENITH	S.	Polite
V - 20. DEBRIS	T.	Full of servile compliance; fawning
D - 21. OGRE	U.	Urged; prodded
P - 22. INCORRIGIBLE	V.	Scattered remains of something broken
J - 23. APEX	W.	Bad or uneasy feeling
G - 24. VINTAGE	X.	Inferior or undesirable dog
L - 25. CONCISE	Y.	Lament; feel or express deep sorrow

Travels With Charley Vocabulary Matching 3

___ 1. DECADENT
___ 2. FRACAS
___ 3. INCORRIGIBLE
___ 4. LACONIC
___ 5. POSTULATE
___ 6. OBSEQUIOUS
___ 7. INALIENABLE
___ 8. INVECTIVES
___ 9. PRECIOUS
___10. CALLOW
___11. KIN
___12. UBIQUITOUS
___13. CONSUMMATE
___14. PARADOX
___15. CORPULENCE
___16. ZENITH
___17. CORROBORATE
___18. NUISANCE
___19. CONDUCIVE
___20. DOCILE
___21. OBLIQUE
___22. TACITURN
___23. DEPLORE
___24. OSTENTATION
___25. APLOMB

A. Teachable; yielding; able to be formed
B. Terse; concise; succinct
C. Helping to bring about an event
D. Lament; feel or express deep sorrow
E. Seemingly contradictory statement that may nonetheless be true
F. Relatives
G. Can't be corrected or reformed
H. Indirect or evasive in meaning or expression; not straightforward
I. Statement generally accepted without proof
J. Abusive, insulting expressions
K. Condition or process of moral decay
L. Skilled; perfect
M. Upper region of the sky
N. Attested to the truth or accuracy of something
O. Noisy quarrel; brawl
P. Valuable
Q. Not talkative
R. A source of inconvenience or bother
S. Immature; inexperienced
T. Poise; self-confidence; assurance
U. Full of servile compliance; fawning
V. Showiness to impress others
W. Being fat
X. Seeming to be everywhere at one time
Y. Absolute; not to be given up

Travels With Charley Vocabulary Matching 3 Answer Key

K - 1. DECADENT	A. Teachable; yielding; able to be formed
O - 2. FRACAS	B. Terse; concise; succinct
G - 3. INCORRIGIBLE	C. Helping to bring about an event
B - 4. LACONIC	D. Lament; feel or express deep sorrow
I - 5. POSTULATE	E. Seemingly contradictory statement that may nonetheless be true
U - 6. OBSEQUIOUS	F. Relatives
Y - 7. INALIENABLE	G. Can't be corrected or reformed
J - 8. INVECTIVES	H. Indirect or evasive in meaning or expression; not straightforward
P - 9. PRECIOUS	I. Statement generally accepted without proof
S - 10. CALLOW	J. Abusive, insulting expressions
F - 11. KIN	K. Condition or process of moral decay
X - 12. UBIQUITOUS	L. Skilled; perfect
L - 13. CONSUMMATE	M. Upper region of the sky
E - 14. PARADOX	N. Attested to the truth or accuracy of something
W - 15. CORPULENCE	O. Noisy quarrel; brawl
M - 16. ZENITH	P. Valuable
N - 17. CORROBORATE	Q. Not talkative
R - 18. NUISANCE	R. A source of inconvenience or bother
C - 19. CONDUCIVE	S. Immature; inexperienced
A - 20. DOCILE	T. Poise; self-confidence; assurance
H - 21. OBLIQUE	U. Full of servile compliance; fawning
Q - 22. TACITURN	V. Showiness to impress others
D - 23. DEPLORE	W. Being fat
V - 24. OSTENTATION	X. Seeming to be everywhere at one time
T - 25. APLOMB	Y. Absolute; not to be given up

Travels With Charley Vocabulary Matching 4

___ 1. CUR
___ 2. UBIQUITOUS
___ 3. COURTEOUS
___ 4. ATROPHIED
___ 5. CONDUCIVE
___ 6. INEPT
___ 7. AVID
___ 8. APHIDS
___ 9. ORGY
___ 10. PRECIOUS
___ 11. CORROBORATE
___ 12. OSTENTATION
___ 13. ANARCHISM
___ 14. CALLOW
___ 15. OBSEQUIOUS
___ 16. DISPEL
___ 17. CONCISE
___ 18. DOCILE
___ 19. OGRE
___ 20. VINTAGE
___ 21. OBLIQUE
___ 22. COERCION
___ 23. DECADENT
___ 24. DEBRIS
___ 25. APEX

A. Small soft-bodied insects that suck sap from plants
B. Indirect or evasive in meaning or expression; not straightforward
C. Helping to bring about an event
D. Eager
E. Anyone especially cruel, brutish, or hideous
F. Scattered remains of something broken
G. Theory that all governments are bad & should be abolished
H. Classic; characterized by enduring appeal
I. Full of servile compliance; fawning
J. Valuable
K. A revel involving unrestrained indulgence
L. Immature; inexperienced
M. Wasted away
N. Teachable; yielding; able to be formed
O. Seeming to be everywhere at one time
P. Attested to the truth or accuracy of something
Q. Expressing much in a few words
R. Highest point; culmination
S. Forcing to think or act in a certain manner by threat or force
T. Inferior or undesirable dog
U. Showiness to impress others
V. Polite
W. Clumsy; incompetent
X. Condition or process of moral decay
Y. To rid of by or as if by driving away or scattering

Travels With Charley Vocabulary Matching 4 Answer Key

T - 1. CUR	A. Small soft-bodied insects that suck sap from plants
O - 2. UBIQUITOUS	B. Indirect or evasive in meaning or expression; not straightforward
V - 3. COURTEOUS	C. Helping to bring about an event
M - 4. ATROPHIED	D. Eager
C - 5. CONDUCIVE	E. Anyone especially cruel, brutish, or hideous
W - 6. INEPT	F. Scattered remains of something broken
D - 7. AVID	G. Theory that all governments are bad & should be abolished
A - 8. APHIDS	H. Classic; characterized by enduring appeal
K - 9. ORGY	I. Full of servile compliance; fawning
J - 10. PRECIOUS	J. Valuable
P - 11. CORROBORATE	K. A revel involving unrestrained indulgence
U - 12. OSTENTATION	L. Immature; inexperienced
G - 13. ANARCHISM	M. Wasted away
L - 14. CALLOW	N. Teachable; yielding; able to be formed
I - 15. OBSEQUIOUS	O. Seeming to be everywhere at one time
Y - 16. DISPEL	P. Attested to the truth or accuracy of something
Q - 17. CONCISE	Q. Expressing much in a few words
N - 18. DOCILE	R. Highest point; culmination
E - 19. OGRE	S. Forcing to think or act in a certain manner by threat or force
H - 20. VINTAGE	T. Inferior or undesirable dog
B - 21. OBLIQUE	U. Showiness to impress others
S - 22. COERCION	V. Polite
X - 23. DECADENT	W. Clumsy; incompetent
F - 24. DEBRIS	X. Condition or process of moral decay
R - 25. APEX	Y. To rid of by or as if by driving away or scattering

Travels With Charley Vocabulary Magic Squares 1

Match the definition with the vocabulary word. Put your answers in the magic squares below. When your answers are correct, all columns and rows will add to the same number.

A. ELATE
B. TAWDRY
C. COURTEOUS
D. APHIDS
E. GALL
F. INEPT
G. CONCISE
H. DECADENT
I. UBIQUITOUS
J. FRACAS
K. COERCION
L. PREMISE
M. SEMANTIC
N. OSTENTATION
O. CORPULENCE
P. ZENITH

1. Being fat
2. Noisy quarrel; brawl
3. Condition or process of moral decay
4. Raise the spirits of; make joyful
5. Small soft-bodied insects that suck sap from plants
6. Nerve; impudence
7. Forcing to think or act in a certain manner by threat or force
8. Showiness to impress others
9. Clumsy; incompetent
10. Polite
11. Relating to language
12. Statement on which an argument is based or from which a conclusion is drawn
13. Seeming to be everywhere at one time
14. Upper region of the sky
15. Gaudy & cheap
16. Expressing much in a few words

A=	B=	C=	D=
E=	F=	G=	H=
I=	J=	K=	L=
M=	N=	O=	P=

Travels With Charley Vocabulary Magic Squares 1 Answer Key

Match the definition with the vocabulary word. Put your answers in the magic squares below. When your answers are correct, all columns and rows will add to the same number.

A. ELATE
B. TAWDRY
C. COURTEOUS
D. APHIDS
E. GALL
F. INEPT
G. CONCISE
H. DECADENT
I. UBIQUITOUS
J. FRACAS
K. COERCION
L. PREMISE
M. SEMANTIC
N. OSTENTATION
O. CORPULENCE
P. ZENITH

1. Being fat
2. Noisy quarrel; brawl
3. Condition or process of moral decay
4. Raise the spirits of; make joyful
5. Small soft-bodied insects that suck sap from plants
6. Nerve; impudence
7. Forcing to think or act in a certain manner by threat or force
8. Showiness to impress others
9. Clumsy; incompetent
10. Polite
11. Relating to language
12. Statement on which an argument is based or from which a conclusion is drawn
13. Seeming to be everywhere at one time
14. Upper region of the sky
15. Gaudy & cheap
16. Expressing much in a few words

A=4	B=15	C=10	D=5
E=6	F=9	G=16	H=3
I=13	J=2	K=7	L=12
M=11	N=8	O=1	P=14

Travels With Charley Vocabulary Magic Squares 2

Match the definition with the vocabulary word. Put your answers in the magic squares below. When your answers are correct, all columns and rows will add to the same number.

A. OBLIQUE
B. OGRE
C. CONSUMMATE
D. ANARCHISM
E. COURTEOUS
F. CORPULENCE
G. LACONIC
H. PANDEMONIUM
I. CONCISE
J. DISPEL
K. AESTHETIC
L. VICARIOUS
M. SUBTLETIES
N. PARADOX
O. INCORRIGIBLE
P. DEPLORE

1. Can't be corrected or reformed
2. Theory that all governments are bad & should be abolished
3. To rid of by or as if by driving away or scattering
4. Polite
5. Expressing much in a few words
6. Being fat
7. Lament; feel or express deep sorrow
8. Skilled; perfect
9. Uproar & noise
10. Pertaining to the sense of beauty
11. Indirect or evasive in meaning or expression; not straightforward
12. Seemingly contradictory statement that may nonetheless be true
13. Anyone especially cruel, brutish, or hideous
14. Details; refinements
15. Terse; concise; succinct
16. Experienced through imaginative participation in the experiences of others others

A=	B=	C=	D=
E=	F=	G=	H=
I=	J=	K=	L=
M=	N=	O=	P=

Travels With Charley Vocabulary Magic Squares 2 Answer Key

Match the definition with the vocabulary word. Put your answers in the magic squares below. When your answers are correct, all columns and rows will add to the same number.

A. OBLIQUE
B. OGRE
C. CONSUMMATE
D. ANARCHISM
E. COURTEOUS
F. CORPULENCE
G. LACONIC
H. PANDEMONIUM
I. CONCISE
J. DISPEL
K. AESTHETIC
L. VICARIOUS
M. SUBTLETIES
N. PARADOX
O. INCORRIGIBLE
P. DEPLORE

1. Can't be corrected or reformed
2. Theory that all governments are bad & should be abolished
3. To rid of by or as if by driving away or scattering
4. Polite
5. Expressing much in a few words
6. Being fat
7. Lament; feel or express deep sorrow
8. Skilled; perfect
9. Uproar & noise
10. Pertaining to the sense of beauty
11. Indirect or evasive in meaning or expression; not straightforward
12. Seemingly contradictory statement that may nonetheless be true
13. Anyone especially cruel, brutish, or hideous
14. Details; refinements
15. Terse; concise; succinct
16. Experienced through imaginative participation in the experiences of others others

A=11	B=13	C=8	D=2
E=4	F=6	G=15	H=9
I=5	J=3	K=10	L=16
M=14	N=12	O=1	P=7

Travels With Charley Vocabulary Magic Squares 3

Match the definition with the vocabulary word. Put your answers in the magic squares below. When your answers are correct, all columns and rows will add to the same number.

A. OGRE
B. SEMANTIC
C. PANDEMONIUM
D. ZENITH
E. OBLIQUE
F. MISANTHROPY
G. VINTAGE
H. TRAVAIL
I. INCISED
J. CONSUMMATE
K. ANARCHISM
L. PERIPATETIC
M. KIN
N. OSTENTATION
O. ELATE
P. APHIDS

1. Relatives
2. Hatred of mankind
3. Labor
4. Raise the spirits of; make joyful
5. Roaming; wandering
6. Uproar & noise
7. Anyone especially cruel, brutish, or hideous
8. Skilled; perfect
9. Theory that all governments are bad & should be abolished
10. Upper region of the sky
11. Relating to language
12. Cut into
13. Showiness to impress others
14. Indirect or evasive in meaning or expression; not straightforward
15. Classic; characterized by enduring appeal
16. Small soft-bodied insects that suck sap from plants

A=	B=	C=	D=
E=	F=	G=	H=
I=	J=	K=	L=
M=	N=	O=	P=

Travels With Charley Vocabulary Magic Squares 3 Answer Key

Match the definition with the vocabulary word. Put your answers in the magic squares below. When your answers are correct, all columns and rows will add to the same number.

A. OGRE
B. SEMANTIC
C. PANDEMONIUM
D. ZENITH
E. OBLIQUE
F. MISANTHROPY
G. VINTAGE
H. TRAVAIL
I. INCISED
J. CONSUMMATE
K. ANARCHISM
L. PERIPATETIC
M. KIN
N. OSTENTATION
O. ELATE
P. APHIDS

1. Relatives
2. Hatred of mankind
3. Labor
4. Raise the spirits of; make joyful
5. Roaming; wandering
6. Uproar & noise
7. Anyone especially cruel, brutish, or hideous
8. Skilled; perfect
9. Theory that all governments are bad & should be abolished
10. Upper region of the sky
11. Relating to language
12. Cut into
13. Showiness to impress others
14. Indirect or evasive in meaning or expression; not straightforward
15. Classic; characterized by enduring appeal
16. Small soft-bodied insects that suck sap from plants

A=7	B=11	C=6	D=10
E=14	F=2	G=15	H=3
I=12	J=8	K=9	L=5
M=1	N=13	O=4	P=16

Travels With Charley Vocabulary Magic Squares 4

Match the definition with the vocabulary word. Put your answers in the magic squares below. When your answers are correct, all columns and rows will add to the same number.

A. INALIENABLE
B. PRECIOUS
C. ANTIDOTE
D. CONCISE
E. AESTHETIC
F. AVID
G. NUISANCE
H. CONDUCIVE
I. SEMANTIC
J. CLOISTERED
K. CALLOW
L. ATROPHIED
M. OBSEQUIOUS
N. VINTAGE
O. VICARIOUS
P. COURTEOUS

1. Helping to bring about an event
2. Full of servile compliance; fawning
3. Valuable
4. Immature; inexperienced
5. Sheltered
6. Anything that relieves or counteracts an injurious effect
7. Polite
8. Pertaining to the sense of beauty
9. Experienced through imaginative participation in the experiences of others
10. Eager
11. Relating to language
12. Expressing much in a few words
13. Absolute; not to be given up
14. Wasted away
15. A source of inconvenience or bother
16. Classic; characterized by enduring appeal

A=	B=	C=	D=
E=	F=	G=	H=
I=	J=	K=	L=
M=	N=	O=	P=

Travels With Charley Vocabulary Magic Squares 4 Answer Key

Match the definition with the vocabulary word. Put your answers in the magic squares below. When your answers are correct, all columns and rows will add to the same number.

A. INALIENABLE
B. PRECIOUS
C. ANTIDOTE
D. CONCISE
E. AESTHETIC
F. AVID

G. NUISANCE
H. CONDUCIVE
I. SEMANTIC
J. CLOISTERED
K. CALLOW
L. ATROPHIED

M. OBSEQUIOUS
N. VINTAGE
O. VICARIOUS
P. COURTEOUS

1. Helping to bring about an event
2. Full of servile compliance; fawning
3. Valuable
4. Immature; inexperienced
5. Sheltered
6. Anything that relieves or counteracts an injurious effect
7. Polite
8. Pertaining to the sense of beauty
9. Experienced through imaginative participation in the experiences of others
10. Eager
11. Relating to language
12. Expressing much in a few words
13. Absolute; not to be given up
14. Wasted away
15. A source of inconvenience or bother
16. Classic; characterized by enduring appeal

A=13	B=3	C=6	D=12
E=8	F=10	G=15	H=1
I=11	J=5	K=4	L=14
M=2	N=16	O=9	P=7

Travels With Charley Vocabulary Word Search 1

Words are placed backwards, forward, diagonally, up and down. Clues listed below can help you find the words. Circle the hidden vocabulary words in the maze.

```
O P A R A D O X Z Y V D E D A O G X
B R Y S K H D S O A P T S G H S Z F
S S S K G I F V N P A Q I K E T E H
O R G Y J X N Y S L D O C I L E N B
L K P R O E R I U O H K N Q B N I G
E S H D G Y E T W M R N O D I T T Q
S S R W R G S M D B B Z C D G A H X
C U R A E O S E M A N T I C I T A H
E O D T P Y B D Q B B S N Z R I V V
N I N H K R T I U M P E A T R O I M
C C O D I H B O A E L R L Y O N D G
E E B S U C N C L W A W I L C G V B
A R S A I C O R M F C V E E N A I G
P P E C L N I E S S O I N U I L C D
E C Q A I L C V V I N T A G E L A K
X A U R A N R I E K I A B A T W R F
M L I F V X E M S L C L L V D P I V
S L O K A W O P W E A I E L T R O Q
N O U X R P C R T Z D T E S V G U V
Z W S E T O D I T N A Y E M G B S P
```

A revel involving unrestrained indulgence (4)
Absolute; not to be given up (11)
Anyone especially cruel, brutish, or hideous (4)
Anything that relieves or counteracts an injurious effect (8)
Attack (5)
Bad or uneasy feeling (6)
Being replaced by something newer (12)
Can't be corrected or reformed (12)
Classic; characterized by enduring appeal (7)
Clumsy; incompetent (5)
Cut into (7)
Eager (4)
Energy; liveliness (8)
Experienced through imaginative participation in the experiences of others (9)
Expressing much in a few words (7)
Forcing to think or act in a certain manner by threat or force (8)
Full of servile compliance; fawning (10)
Gaudy & cheap (6)
Helping to bring about an event (9)
Highest point; culmination (4)
Immature; inexperienced (6)
Inferior or undesirable dog (3)

Labor (7)
Messenger (5)
Neither good or bad; average; ordinary (8)
Nerve; impudence (4)
Noisy quarrel; brawl (6)
Not clearly expressed or defined (7)
Poise; self-confidence; assurance (6)
Raise the spirits of; make joyful (5)
Relating to language (8)
Relatives (3)
Scattered remains of something broken (6)
Seemingly contradictory statement that may nonetheless be true (7)
Showiness to impress others (11)
Statement generally accepted without proof (9)
Teachable; yielding; able to be formed (6)
Terse; concise; succinct (7)
To obtain forcefully (5)
To rid of by or as if by driving away or scattering (6)
Upper region of the sky (6)
Urged; prodded (6)
Valuable (8)
Wasting time lingering (6)

Travels With Charley Vocabulary Word Search 1 Answer Key

Words are placed backwards, forward, diagonally, up and down. Clues listed below can help you find the words. Circle the hidden vocabulary words in the maze.

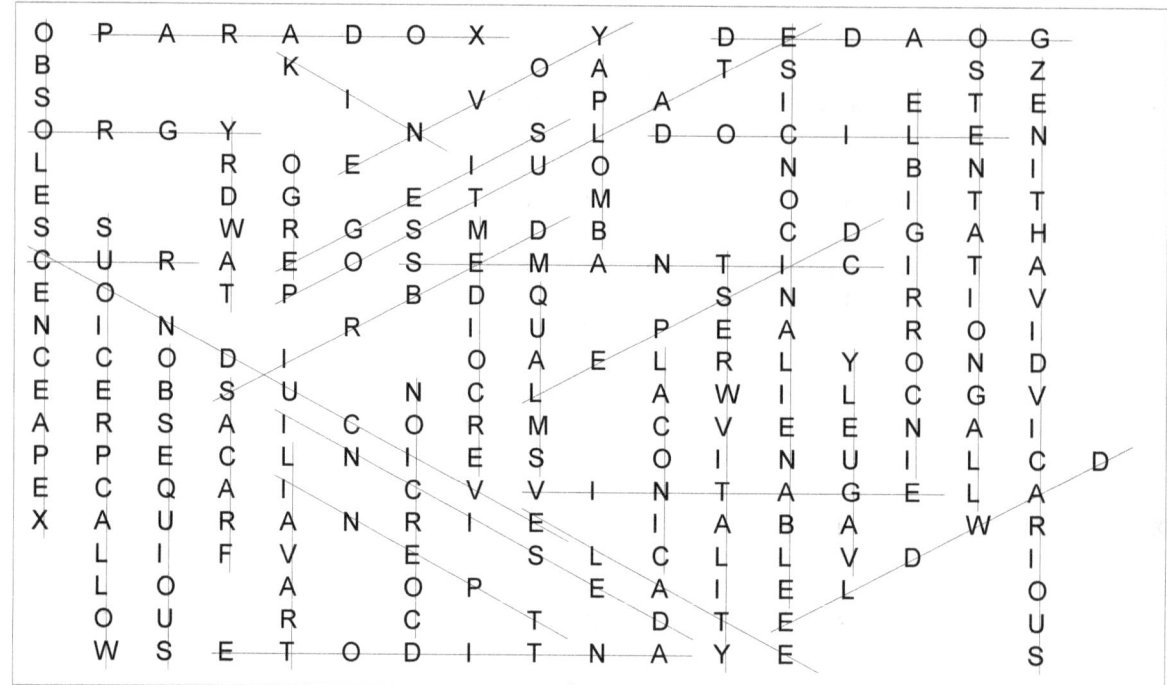

A revel involving unrestrained indulgence (4)
Absolute; not to be given up (11)
Anyone especially cruel, brutish, or hideous (4)
Anything that relieves or counteracts an injurious effect (8)
Attack (5)
Bad or uneasy feeling (6)
Being replaced by something newer (12)
Can't be corrected or reformed (12)
Classic; characterized by enduring appeal (7)
Clumsy; incompetent (5)
Cut into (7)
Eager (4)
Energy; liveliness (8)
Experienced through imaginative participation in the experiences of others (9)
Expressing much in a few words (7)
Forcing to think or act in a certain manner by threat or force (8)
Full of servile compliance; fawning (10)
Gaudy & cheap (6)
Helping to bring about an event (9)
Highest point; culmination (4)
Immature; inexperienced (6)
Inferior or undesirable dog (3)

Labor (7)
Messenger (5)
Neither good or bad; average; ordinary (8)
Nerve; impudence (4)
Noisy quarrel; brawl (6)
Not clearly expressed or defined (7)
Poise; self-confidence; assurance (6)
Raise the spirits of; make joyful (5)
Relating to language (8)
Relatives (3)
Scattered remains of something broken (6)
Seemingly contradictory statement that may nonetheless be true (7)
Showiness to impress others (11)
Statement generally accepted without proof (9)
Teachable; yielding; able to be formed (6)
Terse; concise; succinct (7)
To obtain forcefully (5)
To rid of by or as if by driving away or scattering (6)
Upper region of the sky (6)
Urged; prodded (6)
Valuable (8)
Wasting time lingering (6)

Travels With Charley Vocabulary Word Search 2

Words are placed backwards, forward, diagonally, up and down. Clues listed below can help you find the words. Circle the hidden vocabulary words in the maze.

```
D N O I T A T N E T S O K I N O S R
E E D Y P A P A Q C R B Y T T R E Z
P Q B K Z R C Y W G O A W P P G M L
L O G R E G T I O D P N V P E Y A V
O S L M I I V A T H R R D A N T N H
R Q I G L S D N S U P Y E U I K T K
E S S A K E W T H B R A N C C L I S
E J T U D Z B I W V X N R X I I C H
R I N C B M E D I O C R E A R O V Z
V R U T V T X O I I R T D L D D U E
S D I H P A L T T N F O Z A E O T S
S I S S I E G E S I C N O C P S X L
R S A X W K T E T I Y I A O E E M L
L P N P T A T L L I L D S R Z L X J
L E C M P A B E S J E T W E G A E H
A L E I L M R A Y N U S O L D C N Y
G V R E O U C F T L G T L D N O V R
T E I L C A T M A F A K L W Q N O G
P M P D R K F T V P V S A A G I Y T
B A J F C O E R C I O N C D D C R Y
```

A revel involving unrestrained indulgence (4)
A source of inconvenience or bother (8)
Anyone especially cruel, brutish, or hideous (4)
Anything that relieves or counteracts an injurious effect (8)
Attack (5)
Clumsy; incompetent (5)
Condition or process of moral decay (8)
Cut into (7)
Details; refinements (10)
Eager (4)
Energy; liveliness (8)
Expressing much in a few words (7)
Forcing to think or act in a certain manner by threat or force (8)
Gaudy & cheap (6)
Helping to bring about an event (9)
Highest point; culmination (4)
Immature; inexperienced (6)
Inferior or undesirable dog (3)
Labor (7)
Lament; feel or express deep sorrow (7)
Messenger (5)
Neither good or bad; average; ordinary (8)
Nerve; impudence (4)

Noisy quarrel; brawl (6)
Not clearly expressed or defined (7)
Not talkative (8)
Poise; self-confidence; assurance (6)
Raise the spirits of; make joyful (5)
Relating to language (8)
Relatives (3)
Roaming; wandering (11)
Scattered remains of something broken (6)
Seemingly contradictory statement that may nonetheless be true (7)
Showiness to impress others (11)
Small soft-bodied insects that suck sap from plants (6)
Statement generally accepted without proof (9)
Statement on which an argument is based or from which a conclusion is drawn (7)
Teachable; yielding; able to be formed (6)
Terse; concise; succinct (7)
To obtain forcefully (5)
To rid of by or as if by driving away or scattering (6)
Urged; prodded (6)
Valuable (8)
Wasting time lingering (6)

Travels With Charley Vocabulary Word Search 2 Answer Key

Words are placed backwards, forward, diagonally, up and down. Clues listed below can help you find the words. Circle the hidden vocabulary words in the maze.

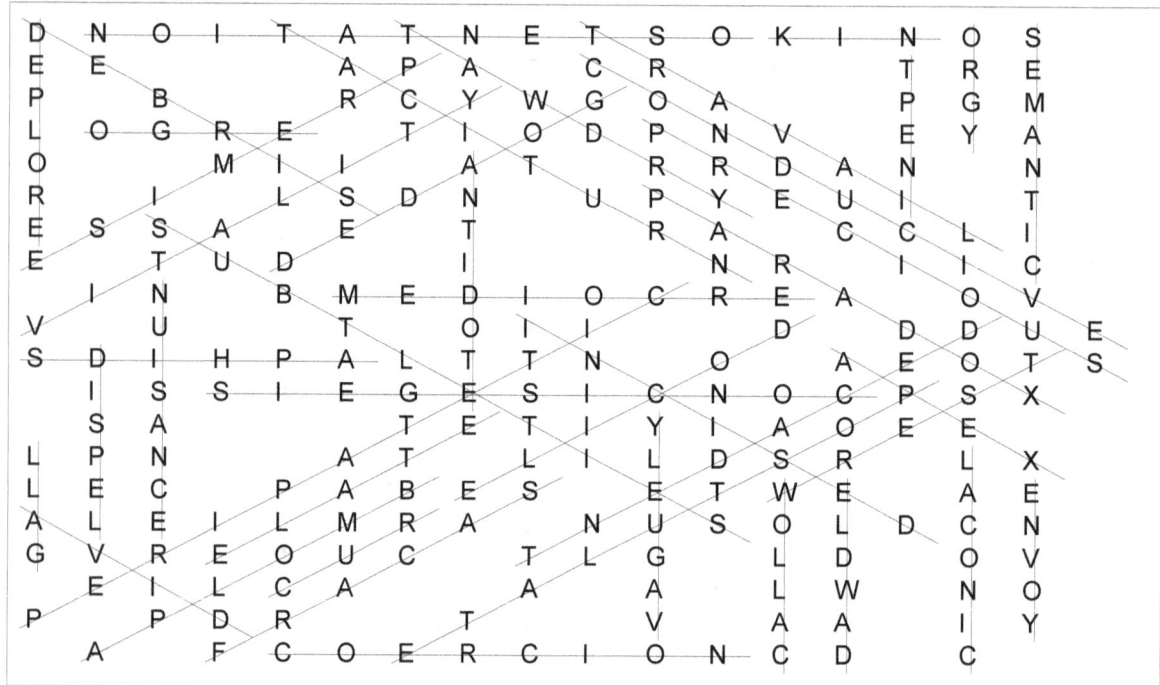

A revel involving unrestrained indulgence (4)
A source of inconvenience or bother (8)
Anyone especially cruel, brutish, or hideous (4)
Anything that relieves or counteracts an injurious effect (8)
Attack (5)
Clumsy; incompetent (5)
Condition or process of moral decay (8)
Cut into (7)
Details; refinements (10)
Eager (4)
Energy; liveliness (8)
Expressing much in a few words (7)
Forcing to think or act in a certain manner by threat or force (8)
Gaudy & cheap (6)
Helping to bring about an event (9)
Highest point; culmination (4)
Immature; inexperienced (6)
Inferior or undesirable dog (3)
Labor (7)
Lament; feel or express deep sorrow (7)
Messenger (5)
Neither good or bad; average; ordinary (8)
Nerve; impudence (4)

Noisy quarrel; brawl (6)
Not clearly expressed or defined (7)
Not talkative (8)
Poise; self-confidence; assurance (6)
Raise the spirits of; make joyful (5)
Relating to language (8)
Relatives (3)
Roaming; wandering (11)
Scattered remains of something broken (6)
Seemingly contradictory statement that may nonetheless be true (7)
Showiness to impress others (11)
Small soft-bodied insects that suck sap from plants (6)
Statement generally accepted without proof (9)
Statement on which an argument is based or from which a conclusion is drawn (7)
Teachable; yielding; able to be formed (6)
Terse; concise; succinct (7)
To obtain forcefully (5)
To rid of by or as if by driving away or scattering (6)
Urged; prodded (6)
Valuable (8)
Wasting time lingering (6)

Travels With Charley Vocabulary Word Search 3

Words are placed backwards, forward, diagonally, up and down. Words listed below are included in the maze. Circle the hidden vocabulary words in the maze.

```
C O N D U C I V E T L E L D W A D J
O M E D I O C R E S A X T Q G T P B
B N U I S A N C E P C W R Y R R R K
L V G Y Y K Q M C P C E D Q Z O E V
I S U O I R A C I V L Z S R T P M V
Q C V H H N L H I B Q E Y A Y H I S
U N B F T Z O T I S N N V Q C I S L
E G E I S S A G A N T I D O T E E J
D L C N T L I O R K D T R H L D C S
Y T A P I R D A D E C H U I N P N S
M Q E T R A I D E P S A C A R F E P
G N Y O E P S E B R A O A J M R C C
I W C L T L P D R E D R N P O W S P
B N L Q A O E E I C O W A L E D E Y
I A W U C M L N S I T R P D G X L K
G L O A I B I I Z O C E G P O E O S
L Y L L T K C C D U D S Y Y U X S W
V D L M U B M S V S F T P G R N B G
K C A S R T W I V I N T A G E L O P
L A C O N I C P C W J V A P H I D S
```

ANTIDOTE	ENVOY	PISCINE
APEX	FRACAS	PRECIOUS
APHIDS	GALL	PREMISE
APLOMB	GOADED	QUALMS
ATROPHIED	INCORRIGIBLE	SEMANTIC
AVID	INEPT	SIEGE
CALLOW	KIN	TACITURN
CONDUCIVE	LACONIC	TAWDRY
CUR	MEDIOCRE	VAGUELY
DAWDLE	NUISANCE	VICARIOUS
DEBRIS	OBLIQUE	VINTAGE
DEPLORE	OBSOLESCENCE	VITALITY
DISPEL	OGRE	WREST
DOCILE	ORGY	ZENITH
ELATE	PARADOX	

Travels With Charley Vocabulary Word Search 3 Answer Key

Words are placed backwards, forward, diagonally, up and down. Words listed below are included in the maze. Circle the hidden vocabulary words in the maze.

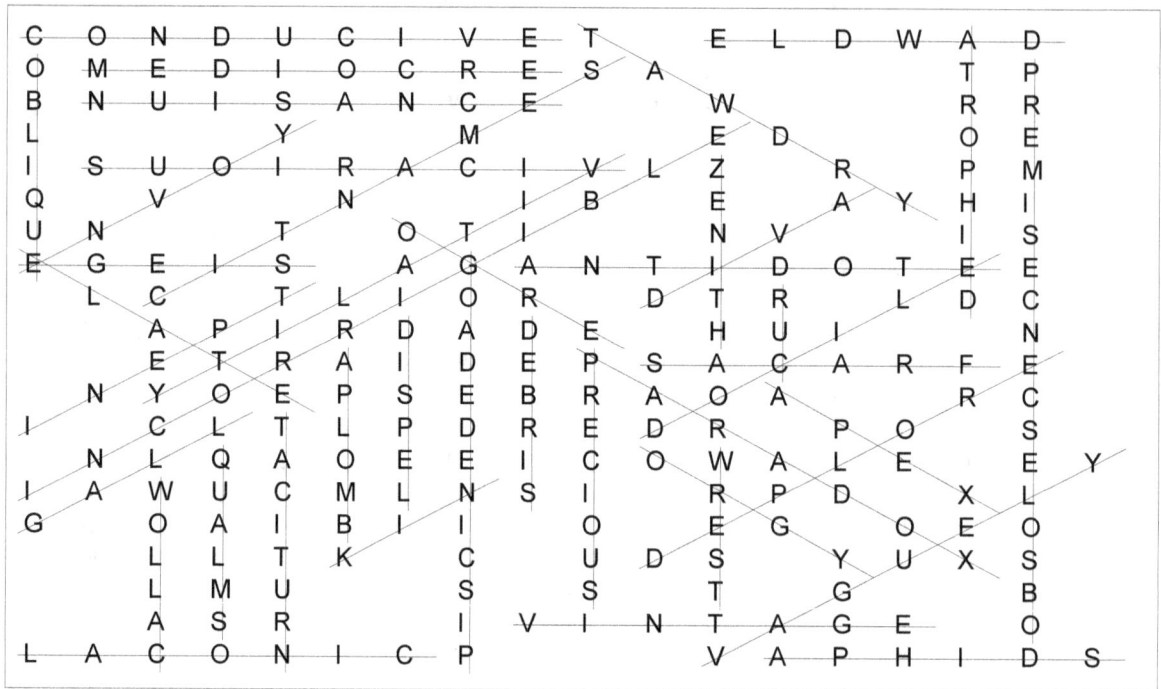

ANTIDOTE	ENVOY	PISCINE
APEX	FRACAS	PRECIOUS
APHIDS	GALL	PREMISE
APLOMB	GOADED	QUALMS
ATROPHIED	INCORRIGIBLE	SEMANTIC
AVID	INEPT	SIEGE
CALLOW	KIN	TACITURN
CONDUCIVE	LACONIC	TAWDRY
CUR	MEDIOCRE	VAGUELY
DAWDLE	NUISANCE	VICARIOUS
DEBRIS	OBLIQUE	VINTAGE
DEPLORE	OBSOLESCENCE	VITALITY
DISPEL	OGRE	WREST
DOCILE	ORGY	ZENITH
ELATE	PARADOX	

Travels With Charley Vocabulary Word Search 4

Words are placed backwards, forward, diagonally, up and down. Words listed below are included in the maze. Circle the hidden vocabulary words in the maze.

```
D I S P E L D W A D E D A O G Q P Z
I N P O G R E L F R A C A S G Z A H
M N K S I E G E S Y N H C U R J N G
E M V T Z K X N M E P Z M B H F D K
D W R E S T U X P R M Z H T I N E Z
I E Q N C I Y L E U G A V L Z T M B
O C C T S T M M Q L L P N E R M O E
C T R A V A I L K A A N W T K I N W
R G N T D S C V C K P T P I I I I M
E C V I E E O O E P E E E E C C U W
E A I O L R N J D S N Y X S V T M H
M W N N G I C T K I V B I C I A C G
G O T A C D I O L R O P I A C C O S
A B A A R S S R E C Y T V L A I N Z
L L G P M C E G R R E V N L R T D P
L I E L H R H Y F H C V D O I U U Q
Q Q A O V I S I T A V I D W O R C N
G U F M V Q D S S K R W O B U N I G
Q E B B N M E S P M S X W N S X V Z
C N G T T A O B S E Q U I O U S E T
```

AESTHETIC	ENVOY	PANDEMONIUM
ANARCHISM	FRACAS	PISCINE
APEX	GALL	PREMISE
APHIDS	GOADED	QUALMS
APLOMB	INEPT	SEMANTIC
AVID	INVECTIVES	SIEGE
CALLOW	KIN	SUBTLETIES
COERCION	LACONIC	TACITURN
CONCISE	MEDIOCRE	TRAVAIL
CONDUCIVE	NUISANCE	VAGUELY
CUR	OBLIQUE	VICARIOUS
DAWDLE	OBSEQUIOUS	VINTAGE
DECADENT	OGRE	WREST
DISPEL	ORGY	ZENITH
ELATE	OSTENTATION	

Travels With Charley Vocabulary Word Search 4 Answer Key

Words are placed backwards, forward, diagonally, up and down. Words listed below are included in the maze. Circle the hidden vocabulary words in the maze.

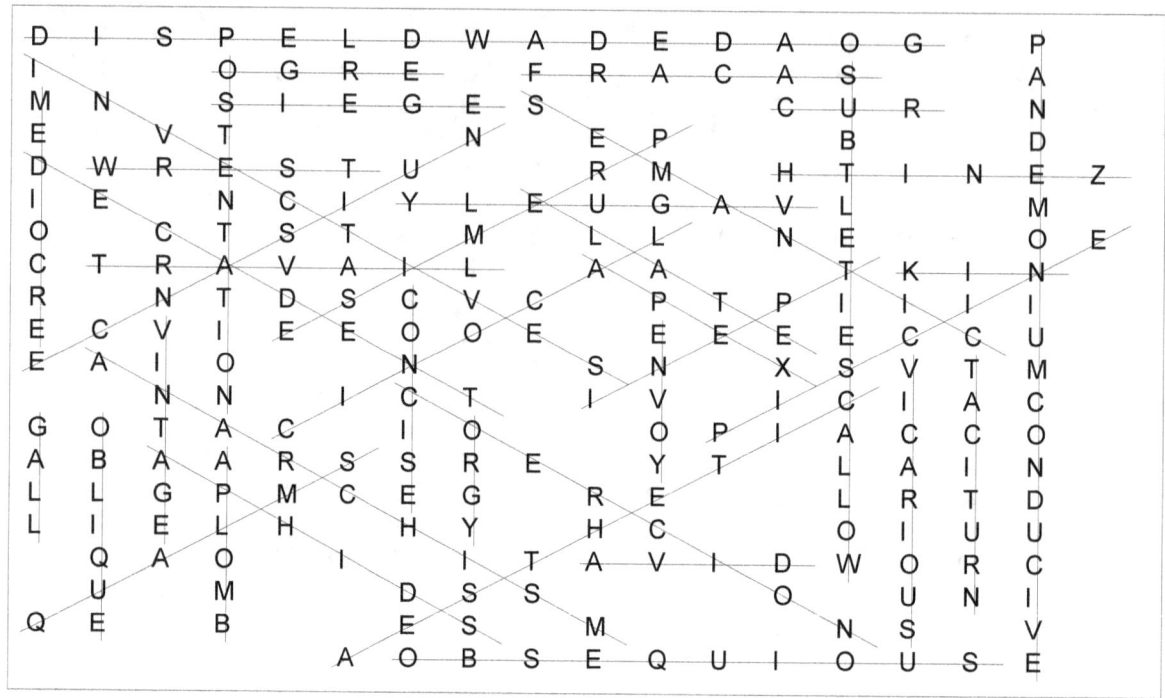

AESTHETIC	ENVOY	PANDEMONIUM
ANARCHISM	FRACAS	PISCINE
APEX	GALL	PREMISE
APHIDS	GOADED	QUALMS
APLOMB	INEPT	SEMANTIC
AVID	INVECTIVES	SIEGE
CALLOW	KIN	SUBTLETIES
COERCION	LACONIC	TACITURN
CONCISE	MEDIOCRE	TRAVAIL
CONDUCIVE	NUISANCE	VAGUELY
CUR	OBLIQUE	VICARIOUS
DAWDLE	OBSEQUIOUS	VINTAGE
DECADENT	OGRE	WREST
DISPEL	ORGY	ZENITH
ELATE	OSTENTATION	

Travels With Charley Vocabulary Crossword 1

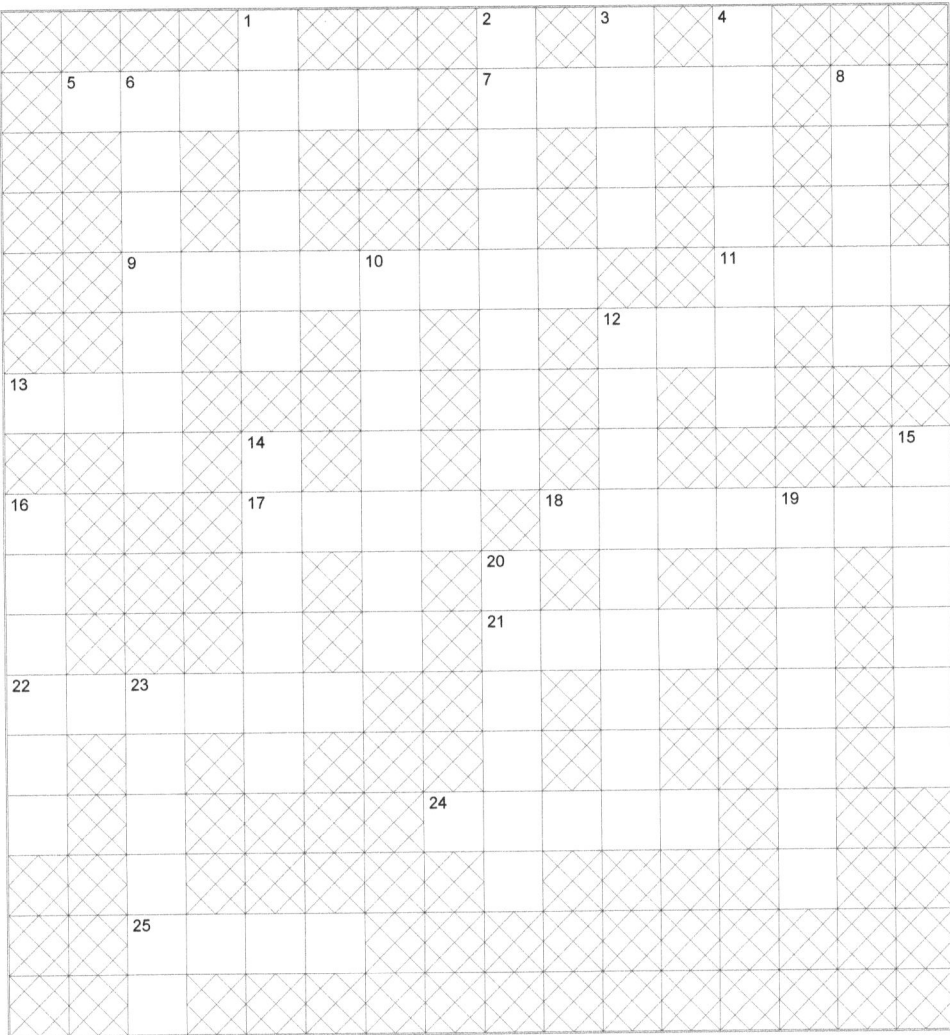

Across
5. Small soft-bodied insects that suck sap from plants
7. Raise the spirits of; make joyful
9. Forcing to think or act in a certain manner by threat or force
11. A revel involving unrestrained indulgence
12. Inferior or undesirable dog
13. Relatives
17. Eager
18. Statement on which an argument is based or from which a conclusion is drawn
21. Highest point; culmination
22. Teachable; yielding; able to be formed
24. To obtain forcefully
25. Anyone especially cruel, brutish, or hideous

Down
1. To rid of by or as if by driving away or scattering
2. Neither good or bad; average; ordinary
3. Nerve; impudence
4. Lament; feel or express deep sorrow
6. Relating to fish
8. Attack
10. Expressing much in a few words
12. Polite
14. Wasting time lingering
15. Scattered remains of something broken
16. Urged; prodded
19. Cut into
20. Gaudy & cheap
23. Immature; inexperienced

Travels With Charley Vocabulary Crossword 1 Answer Key

Across
5. Small soft-bodied insects that suck sap from plants
7. Raise the spirits of; make joyful
9. Forcing to think or act in a certain manner by threat or force
11. A revel involving unrestrained indulgence
12. Inferior or undesirable dog
13. Relatives
17. Eager
18. Statement on which an argument is based or from which a conclusion is drawn
21. Highest point; culmination
22. Teachable; yielding; able to be formed
24. To obtain forcefully
25. Anyone especially cruel, brutish, or hideous

Down
1. To rid of by or as if by driving away or scattering
2. Neither good or bad; average; ordinary
3. Nerve; impudence
4. Lament; feel or express deep sorrow
6. Relating to fish
8. Attack
10. Expressing much in a few words
12. Polite
14. Wasting time lingering
15. Scattered remains of something broken
16. Urged; prodded
19. Cut into
20. Gaudy & cheap
23. Immature; inexperienced

Travels With Charley Vocabulary Crossword 2

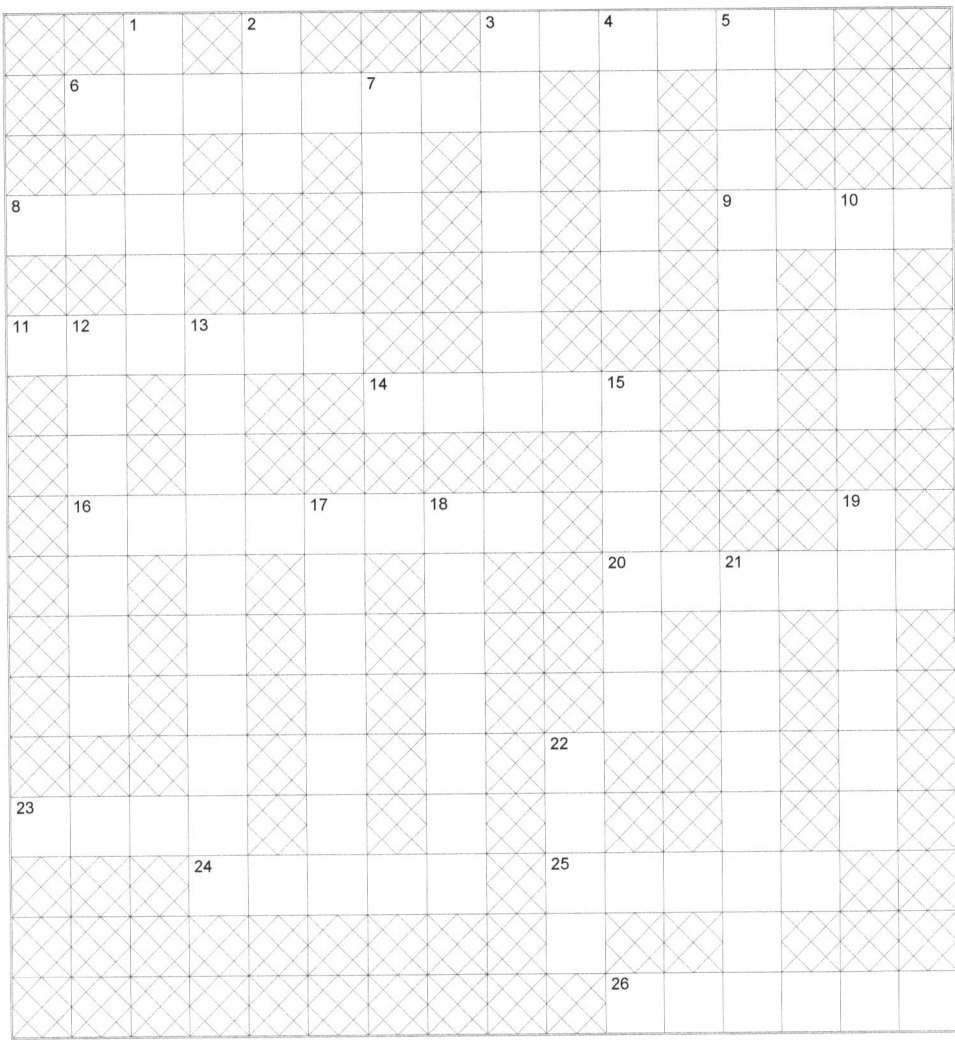

Across
3. Wasting time lingering
6. Neither good or bad; average; ordinary
8. Eager
9. A revel involving unrestrained indulgence
11. Small soft-bodied insects that suck sap from plants
14. Clumsy; incompetent
16. Forcing to think or act in a certain manner by threat or force
20. To rid of by or as if by driving away or scattering
23. Anyone especially cruel, brutish, or hideous
24. Attack
25. Raise the spirits of; make joyful
26. Teachable; yielding; able to be formed

Down
1. Upper region of the sky
2. Relatives
3. Lament; feel or express deep sorrow
4. To obtain forcefully
5. Terse; concise; succinct
7. Inferior or undesirable dog
10. Nerve; impudence
12. Relating to fish
13. Abusive, insulting expressions
15. Gaudy & cheap
17. Expressing much in a few words
18. Indirect or evasive in meaning or expression; not straightforward
19. Scattered remains of something broken
21. Relating to language
22. Highest point; culmination

Travels With Charley Vocabulary Crossword 2 Answer Key

```
        1       2               3   4       5
        Z       K               D   A   W   D   L   E
    6                   7
        M   E   D   I   O   C   R   E       R       A
            N           N           P       E       C
    8                                               9       10
        A   V   I   D           R           L       O   R   G   Y
            T                               O       T       N   A
    11  12      13                  14          15
        A   P   H   I   D   S               R       T       C   L   L
            I           N                   I   N   E   P   T       L
            S           V                           A
            16                  17      18
                C   O   E   R   C   I   O   N       W               19
                                                                    D
                I           C           O                   20  21
                                                            D   I   S   P   E   L
                N           T           N           L                   E       B
                E           I           C           I                   M       R
                                        V           I               22  A
                            V                       Q               A           I
    23
        O   G   R   E           S               U               P               N   S
                        24                                      25
                            S   I   E   G   E                   E   L   A   T   E
                                                                X               I
                                                            26
                                                                D   O   C   I   L   E
```

Across
3. Wasting time lingering
6. Neither good or bad; average; ordinary
8. Eager
9. A revel involving unrestrained indulgence
11. Small soft-bodied insects that suck sap from plants
14. Clumsy; incompetent
16. Forcing to think or act in a certain manner by threat or force
20. To rid of by or as if by driving away or scattering
23. Anyone especially cruel, brutish, or hideous
24. Attack
25. Raise the spirits of; make joyful
26. Teachable; yielding; able to be formed

Down
1. Upper region of the sky
2. Relatives
3. Lament; feel or express deep sorrow
4. To obtain forcefully
5. Terse; concise; succinct
7. Inferior or undesirable dog
10. Nerve; impudence
12. Relating to fish
13. Abusive, insulting expressions
15. Gaudy & cheap
17. Expressing much in a few words
18. Indirect or evasive in meaning or expression; not straightforward
19. Scattered remains of something broken
21. Relating to language
22. Highest point; culmination

Travels With Charley Vocabulary Crossword 3

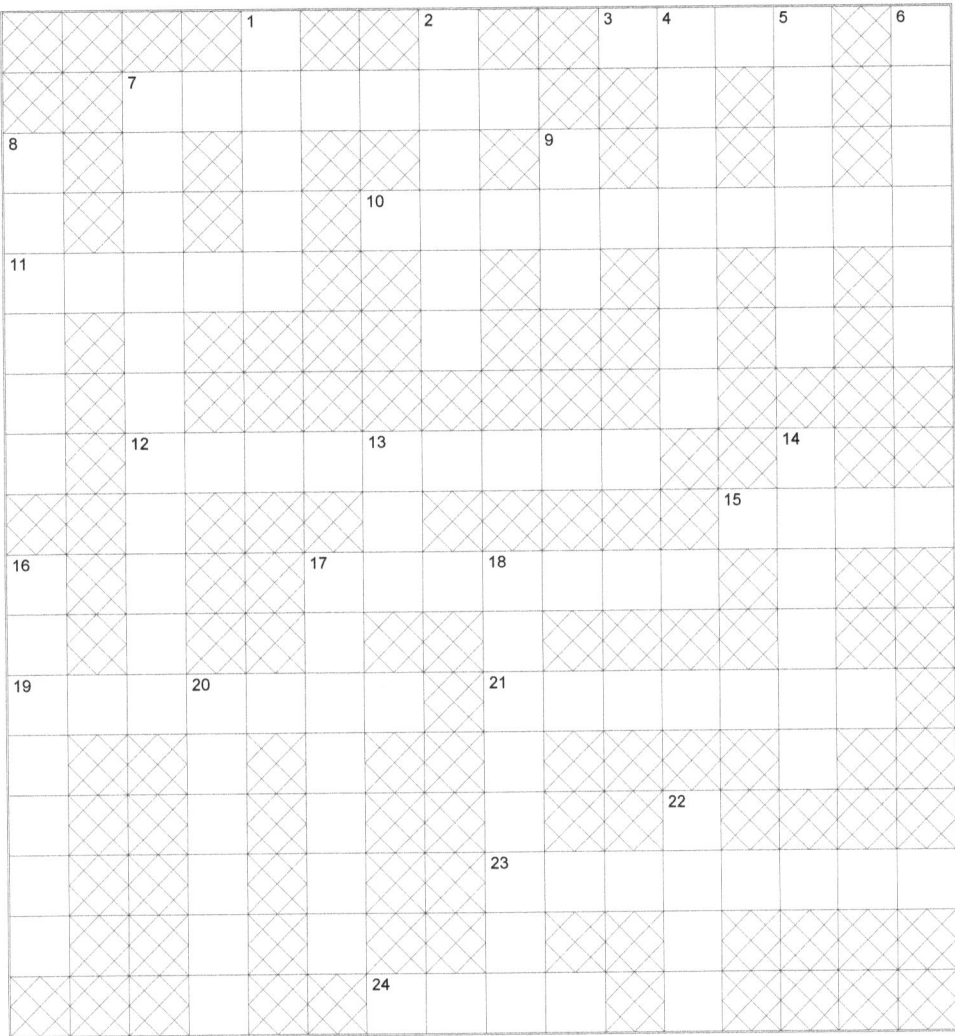

Across
3. Eager
7. Indirect or evasive in meaning or expression; not straightforward
10. Sheltered
11. Attack
12. Theory that all governments are bad & should be abolished
15. Nerve; impudence
17. Statement on which an argument is based or from which a conclusion is drawn
19. Expressing much in a few words
21. Lament; feel or express deep sorrow
23. Forcing to think or act in a certain manner by threat or force
24. Highest point; culmination

Down
1. Raise the spirits of; make joyful
2. Bad or uneasy feeling
4. Classic; characterized by enduring appeal
5. Scattered remains of something broken
6. Wasting time lingering
7. Showiness to impress others
8. To rid of by or as if by driving away or scattering
9. Relatives
13. Inferior or undesirable dog
14. Gaudy & cheap
16. Cut into
17. Relating to fish
18. Neither good or bad; average; ordinary
20. Immature; inexperienced
22. A revel involving unrestrained indulgence

Travels With Charley Vocabulary Crossword 3 Answer Key

			1 E		2 Q		3 A	4 V	I	5 D		6 D
		7 O	B	L	I	Q	U	E		I		E		A
8 D		S		A		A		9 K		N		B	W
I		T		T	10 C	L	O	I	S	T	E	R	E	D
11 S	I	E	G	E		M		N		A		I		L
P		N				S				G		S		E
E		T								E				
L	12 A	N	A	R	13 C	H	I	S	M		14 T		
	T				U					15 G	A	L	L
16 I		17 P	R	18 M	I	S	E		W		
N		O		I		E				D		
19 C	O	20 N	C	I	S	E		21 D	E	P	L	O	R	E
I		A		C				I				Y	
S		L		I				O		22 O		
E		L		N			23 C	O	E	R	C	I	O	N
D		O		E				R		G			
		W			24 A	P	E	X		Y			

Across
3. Eager
7. Indirect or evasive in meaning or expression; not straightforward
10. Sheltered
11. Attack
12. Theory that all governments are bad & should be abolished
15. Nerve; impudence
17. Statement on which an argument is based or from which a conclusion is drawn
19. Expressing much in a few words
21. Lament; feel or express deep sorrow
23. Forcing to think or act in a certain manner by threat or force
24. Highest point; culmination

Down
1. Raise the spirits of; make joyful
2. Bad or uneasy feeling
4. Classic; characterized by enduring appeal
5. Scattered remains of something broken
6. Wasting time lingering
7. Showiness to impress others
8. To rid of by or as if by driving away or scattering
9. Relatives
13. Inferior or undesirable dog
14. Gaudy & cheap
16. Cut into
17. Relating to fish
18. Neither good or bad; average; ordinary
20. Immature; inexperienced
22. A revel involving unrestrained indulgence

Travels With Charley Vocabulary Crossword 4

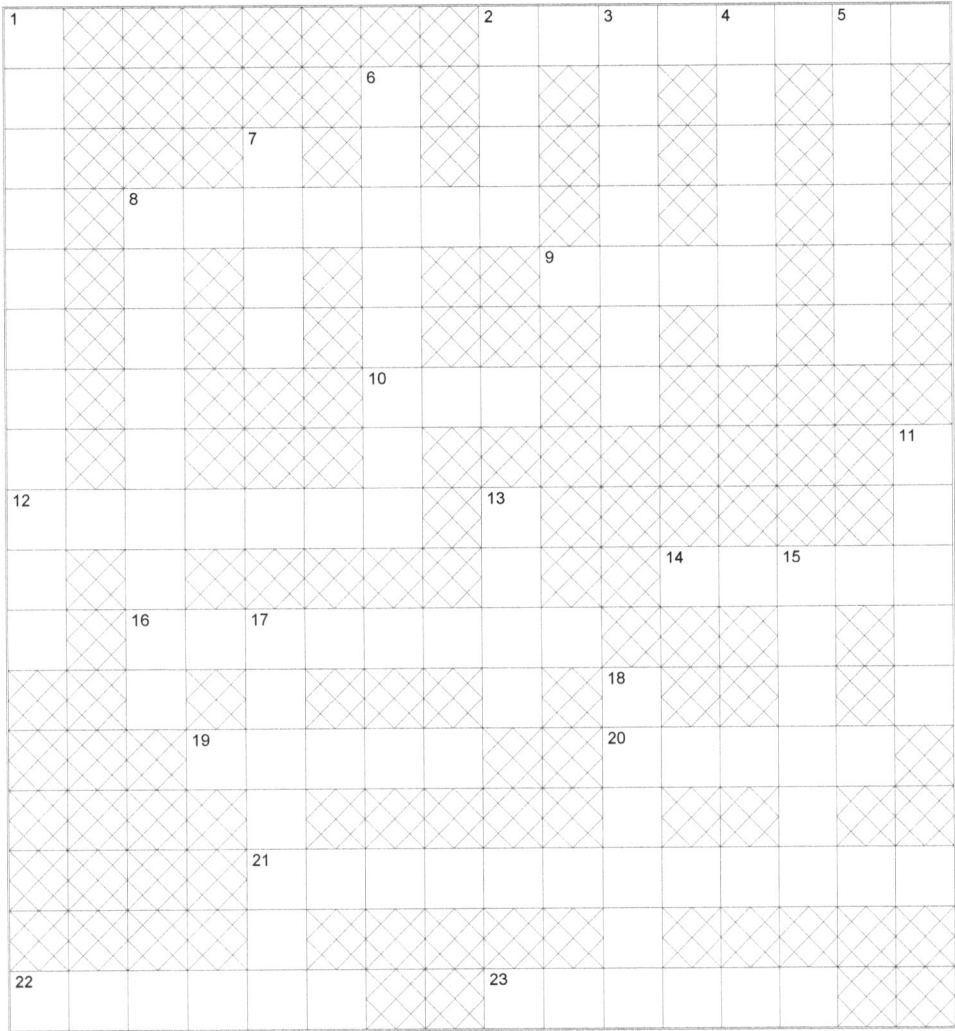

Across
2. Anything that relieves or counteracts an injurious effect
8. Seemingly contradictory statement that may nonetheless be true
9. Nerve; impudence
10. Inferior or undesirable dog
12. Indirect or evasive in meaning or expression; not straightforward
14. Raise the spirits of; make joyful
16. Not talkative
19. Clumsy; incompetent
20. Messenger
21. Can't be corrected or reformed
22. Urged; prodded
23. Small soft-bodied insects that suck sap from plants

Down
1. Hatred of mankind
2. Highest point; culmination
3. Labor
4. Teachable; yielding; able to be formed
5. Gaudy & cheap
6. Neither good or bad; average; ordinary
7. A revel involving unrestrained indulgence
8. Statement generally accepted without proof
11. Attack
13. Anyone especially cruel, brutish, or hideous
15. Poise; self-confidence; assurance
17. Expressing much in a few words
18. Upper region of the sky

Travels With Charley Vocabulary Crossword 4 Answer Key

	1 M						2 A	3 N	T	4 I	D	5 O	T	E
	I				6 M		P		R		O		A	
	S		7 O		E		P		R		O		A	
	S		7 O		E		E		A		C		W	
	A	8 P	A	R	A	D	O	X		V		I		D
	N		O		G		I		9 G	A	L	L		R
	T		S		Y		O			L		E		Y
	H		T			10 C	U	R		L				
	R		U			R							11 S
12 O	B	L	I	Q	U	E		13 O					I
	P		A					G			14 E	15 L	A	T	E
	Y		16 T	17 A	C	I	T	U	R	N		P		G
			E		O			E		18 Z		L		E
				19 I	N	E	P	T		20 E	N	V	O	Y
					C					N		M		
				21 I	N	C	O	R	R	I	G	I	B	L	E
					S					T				
22 G	O	A	D	E	D		23 A	P	H	I	D	S		

Across

2. Anything that relieves or counteracts an injurious effect
8. Seemingly contradictory statement that may nonetheless be true
9. Nerve; impudence
10. Inferior or undesirable dog
12. Indirect or evasive in meaning or expression; not straightforward
14. Raise the spirits of; make joyful
16. Not talkative
19. Clumsy; incompetent
20. Messenger
21. Can't be corrected or reformed
22. Urged; prodded
23. Small soft-bodied insects that suck sap from plants

Down

1. Hatred of mankind
2. Highest point; culmination
3. Labor
4. Teachable; yielding; able to be formed
5. Gaudy & cheap
6. Neither good or bad; average; ordinary
7. A revel involving unrestrained indulgence
8. Statement generally accepted without proof
11. Attack
13. Anyone especially cruel, brutish, or hideous
15. Poise; self-confidence; assurance
17. Expressing much in a few words
18. Upper region of the sky

Travels With Charley Vocabulary Juggle Letters 1

1. EANDTECD = 1. _____
   Condition or process of moral decay

2. LAGL = 2. _____
   Nerve; impudence

3. LOIUQEB = 3. _____
   Indirect or evasive in meaning or expression; not straightforward

4. IBESDR = 4. _____
   Scattered remains of something broken

5. YROG = 5. _____
   A revel involving unrestrained indulgence

6. ILEUTSSTEB = 6. _____
   Details; refinements

7. REGO = 7. _____
   Anyone especially cruel, brutish, or hideous

8. IITVYLAT = 8. _____
   Energy; liveliness

9. SIRUECPO = 9. _____
   Valuable

10. IVTENVESIC =10. _____
    Abusive, insulting expressions

11. EISTCAMN =11. _____
    Relating to language

12. MIUNDANMPOE =12. _____
    Uproar & noise

13. CANIOLC =13. _____
    Terse; concise; succinct

14. IAMARSNHC =14. _____
    Theory that all governments are bad & should be abolished

15. EOVYN =15. _____
    Messenger

Travels With Charley Vocabulary Juggle Letters 1 Answer Key

1. EANDTECD = 1. DECADENT
   Condition or process of moral decay

2. LAGL = 2. GALL
   Nerve; impudence

3. LOIUQEB = 3. OBLIQUE
   Indirect or evasive in meaning or expression; not straightforward

4. IBESDR = 4. DEBRIS
   Scattered remains of something broken

5. YROG = 5. ORGY
   A revel involving unrestrained indulgence

6. ILEUTSSTEB = 6. SUBTLETIES
   Details; refinements

7. REGO = 7. OGRE
   Anyone especially cruel, brutish, or hideous

8. IITVYLAT = 8. VITALITY
   Energy; liveliness

9. SIRUECPO = 9. PRECIOUS
   Valuable

10. IVTENVESIC = 10. INVECTIVES
    Abusive, insulting expressions

11. EISTCAMN = 11. SEMANTIC
    Relating to language

12. MIUNDANMPOE = 12. PANDEMONIUM
    Uproar & noise

13. CANIOLC = 13. LACONIC
    Terse; concise; succinct

14. IAMARSNHC = 14. ANARCHISM
    Theory that all governments are bad & should be abolished

15. EOVYN = 15. ENVOY
    Messenger

Travels With Charley Vocabulary Juggle Letters 2

1. UUTBSIOIQU = 1. _____
   Seeming to be everywhere at one time

2. HIENZT = 2. _____
   Upper region of the sky

3. NIVATGE = 3. _____
   Classic; characterized by enduring appeal

4. ARPXOAD = 4. _____
   Seemingly contradictory statement that may nonetheless be true

5. IEORCEMD = 5. _____
   Neither good or bad; average; ordinary

6. LAIALEBNINE = 6. _____
   Absolute; not to be given up

7. PBMLAO = 7. _____
   Poise; self-confidence; assurance

8. DAGEDO = 8. _____
   Urged; prodded

9. OICSCNE = 9. _____
   Expressing much in a few words

10. ESWTR = 10. _____
    To obtain forcefully

11. STEIEVNICV = 11. _____
    Abusive, insulting expressions

12. RCU = 12. _____
    Inferior or undesirable dog

13. POTSAHMYINR = 13. _____
    Hatred of mankind

14. STECAHIET = 14. _____
    Pertaining to the sense of beauty

15. TTINRUCA = 15. _____
    Not talkative

Travels With Charley Vocabulary Juggle Letters 2 Answer Key

1. UUTBSIOIQU = 1. UBIQUITOUS
   Seeming to be everywhere at one time

2. HIENZT = 2. ZENITH
   Upper region of the sky

3. NIVATGE = 3. VINTAGE
   Classic; characterized by enduring appeal

4. ARPXOAD = 4. PARADOX
   Seemingly contradictory statement that may nonetheless be true

5. IEORCEMD = 5. MEDIOCRE
   Neither good or bad; average; ordinary

6. LAIALEBNINE = 6. INALIENABLE
   Absolute; not to be given up

7. PBMLAO = 7. APLOMB
   Poise; self-confidence; assurance

8. DAGEDO = 8. GOADED
   Urged; prodded

9. OICSCNE = 9. CONCISE
   Expressing much in a few words

10. ESWTR =10. WREST
    To obtain forcefully

11. STEIEVNICV =11. INVECTIVES
    Abusive, insulting expressions

12. RCU =12. CUR
    Inferior or undesirable dog

13. POTSAHMYINR =13. MISANTHROPY
    Hatred of mankind

14. STECAHIET =14. AESTHETIC
    Pertaining to the sense of beauty

15. TTINRUCA =15. TACITURN
    Not talkative

Travels With Charley Vocabulary Juggle Letters 3

1. MIHSAARCN = 1. _____
   Theory that all governments are bad & should be abolished

2. CENIDSI = 2. _____
   Cut into

3. EROEPLD = 3. _____
   Lament; feel or express deep sorrow

4. MLUSQA = 4. _____
   Bad or uneasy feeling

5. NGEIATV = 5. _____
   Classic; characterized by enduring appeal

6. SLDEPI = 6. _____
   To rid of by or as if by driving away or scattering

7. EETICAPITRP = 7. _____
   Roaming; wandering

8. MTNECIAS = 8. _____
   Relating to language

9. ALLG = 9. _____
   Nerve; impudence

10. LCOURNEECP = 10. _____
    Being fat

11. ICRCOONE = 11. _____
    Forcing to think or act in a certain manner by threat or force

12. UOQIEBL = 12. _____
    Indirect or evasive in meaning or expression; not straightforward

13. ERTLIOESDC = 13. _____
    Sheltered

14. VCDCENIOU = 14. _____
    Helping to bring about an event

15. CRPSIINEUO = 15. _____
    Destructive; harmful

Travels With Charley Vocabulary Juggle Letters 3 Answer Key

1. MIHSAARCN = 1. ANARCHISM
   Theory that all governments are bad & should be abolished

2. CENIDSI = 2. INCISED
   Cut into

3. EROEPLD = 3. DEPLORE
   Lament; feel or express deep sorrow

4. MLUSQA = 4. QUALMS
   Bad or uneasy feeling

5. NGEIATV = 5. VINTAGE
   Classic; characterized by enduring appeal

6. SLDEPI = 6. DISPEL
   To rid of by or as if by driving away or scattering

7. EETICAPITRP = 7. PERIPATETIC
   Roaming; wandering

8. MTNECIAS = 8. SEMANTIC
   Relating to language

9. ALLG = 9. GALL
   Nerve; impudence

10. LCOURNEECP = 10. CORPULENCE
    Being fat

11. ICRCOONE = 11. COERCION
    Forcing to think or act in a certain manner by threat or force

12. UOQIEBL = 12. OBLIQUE
    Indirect or evasive in meaning or expression; not straightforward

13. ERTLIOESDC = 13. CLOISTERED
    Sheltered

14. VCDCENIOU = 14. CONDUCIVE
    Helping to bring about an event

15. CRPSIINEUO = 15. PERNICIOUS
    Destructive; harmful

Travels With Charley Vocabulary Juggle Letters 4

1. WDYATR = 1. _____
Gaudy & cheap

2. ENSPIIC = 2. _____
Relating to fish

3. HETTSIACE = 3. _____
Pertaining to the sense of beauty

4. HPRIAEDTO = 4. _____
Wasted away

5. SVCENVTIEI = 5. _____
Abusive, insulting expressions

6. UIAENNSC = 6. _____
A source of inconvenience or bother

7. ALOCLW = 7. _____
Immature; inexperienced

8. ANHMSRCIA = 8. _____
Theory that all governments are bad & should be abolished

9. ROGY = 9. _____
A revel involving unrestrained indulgence

10. RCERBOOOATR =10. _____
Attested to the truth or accuracy of something

11. ESIMTACN =11. _____
Relating to language

12. MBLOAP =12. _____
Poise; self-confidence; assurance

13. IOSEUSUQBO =13. _____
Full of servile compliance; fawning

14. LYGEUAV =14. _____
Not clearly expressed or defined

15. AFSCAR =15. _____
Noisy quarrel; brawl

Travels With Charley Vocabulary Juggle Letters 4 Answer Key

1. WDYATR = 1. TAWDRY
Gaudy & cheap

2. ENSPIIC = 2. PISCINE
Relating to fish

3. HETTSIACE = 3. AESTHETIC
Pertaining to the sense of beauty

4. HPRIAEDTO = 4. ATROPHIED
Wasted away

5. SVCENVTIEI = 5. INVECTIVES
Abusive, insulting expressions

6. UIAENNSC = 6. NUISANCE
A source of inconvenience or bother

7. ALOCLW = 7. CALLOW
Immature; inexperienced

8. ANHMSRCIA = 8. ANARCHISM
Theory that all governments are bad & should be abolished

9. ROGY = 9. ORGY
A revel involving unrestrained indulgence

10. RCERBOOOATR =10. CORROBORATE
Attested to the truth or accuracy of something

11. ESIMTACN =11. SEMANTIC
Relating to language

12. MBLOAP =12. APLOMB
Poise; self-confidence; assurance

13. IOSEUSUQBO =13. OBSEQUIOUS
Full of servile compliance; fawning

14. LYGEUAV =14. VAGUELY
Not clearly expressed or defined

15. AFSCAR =15. FRACAS
Noisy quarrel; brawl

AESTHETIC	Pertaining to the sense of beauty
ANARCHISM	Theory that all governments are bad & should be abolished
ANTIDOTE	Anything that relieves or counteracts an injurious effect
APEX	Highest point; culmination
APHIDS	Small soft-bodied insects that suck sap from plants
APLOMB	Poise; self-confidence; assurance

ATROPHIED	Wasted away
AVID	Eager
CALLOW	Immature; inexperienced
CLOISTERED	Sheltered
COERCION	Forcing to think or act in a certain manner by threat or force
CONCISE	Expressing much in a few words

CONDUCIVE	Helping to bring about an event
CONSUMMATE	Skilled; perfect
CORPULENCE	Being fat
CORROBORATE	Attested to the truth or accuracy of something
COURTEOUS	Polite
CUR	Inferior or undesirable dog

DAWDLE	Wasting time lingering
DEBRIS	Scattered remains of something broken
DECADENT	Condition or process of moral decay
DEPLORE	Lament; feel or express deep sorrow
DISPEL	To rid of by or as if by driving away or scattering
DOCILE	Teachable; yielding; able to be formed

ELATE	Raise the spirits of; make joyful
ENVOY	Messenger
FRACAS	Noisy quarrel; brawl
GALL	Nerve; impudence
GOADED	Urged; prodded
INALIENABLE	Absolute; not to be given up

INCISED	Cut into
INCORRIGIBLE	Can't be corrected or reformed
INEPT	Clumsy; incompetent
INVECTIVES	Abusive, insulting expressions
KIN	Relatives
LACONIC	Terse; concise; succinct

MEDIOCRE	Neither good or bad; average; ordinary
MISANTHROPY	Hatred of mankind
NUISANCE	A source of inconvenience or bother
OBLIQUE	Indirect or evasive in meaning or expression; not straightforward
OBSEQUIOUS	Full of servile compliance; fawning
OBSOLESCENCE	Being replaced by something newer

OGRE	Anyone especially cruel, brutish, or hideous
ORGY	A revel involving unrestrained indulgence
OSTENTATION	Showiness to impress others
PANDEMONIUM	Uproar & noise
PARADOX	Seemingly contradictory statement that may nonetheless be true
PERIPATETIC	Roaming; wandering

PERNICIOUS	Destructive; harmful
PISCINE	Relating to fish
POSTULATE	Statement generally accepted without proof
PRECIOUS	Valuable
PREMISE	Statement on which an argument is based or from which a conclusion is drawn
QUALMS	Bad or uneasy feeling

SEMANTIC	Relating to language
SIEGE	Attack
SUBTLETIES	Details; refinements
TACITURN	Not talkative
TAWDRY	Gaudy & cheap
TRAVAIL	Labor

UBIQUITOUS	Seeming to be everywhere at one time
VAGUELY	Not clearly expressed or defined
VICARIOUS	Experienced through imaginative participation in the experiences of others
VINTAGE	Classic; characterized by enduring appeal
VITALITY	Energy; liveliness
WREST	To obtain forcefully

ZENITH | Upper region of the sky

Travels With Charley Vocabular

DAWDLE	OBLIQUE	INCISED	APHIDS	MEDIOCRE
APLOMB	ELATE	APEX	AVID	PREMISE
ANARCHISM	CLOISTERED	FREE SPACE	UBIQUITOUS	DECADENT
ENVOY	ATROPHIED	GALL	PERIPATETIC	ZENITH
PERNICIOUS	ANTIDOTE	PISCINE	SUBTLETIES	PARADOX

Travels With Charley Vocabular

CONCISE	OBSOLESCENCE	DEPLORE	DEBRIS	NUISANCE
CUR	DOCILE	OSTENTATION	INCORRIGIBLE	OGRE
PRECIOUS	VAGUELY	FREE SPACE	TRAVAIL	SIEGE
VINTAGE	QUALMS	VICARIOUS	CORPULENCE	AESTHETIC
GOADED	KIN	LACONIC	CONSUMMATE	POSTULATE

Travels With Charley Vocabular

DAWDLE	PRECIOUS	DECADENT	OSTENTATION	SUBTLETIES
CONCISE	GALL	INEPT	CALLOW	VICARIOUS
OBSOLESCENCE	AVID	FREE SPACE	POSTULATE	VITALITY
AESTHETIC	APHIDS	COERCION	PARADOX	SEMANTIC
PERIPATETIC	VINTAGE	ANTIDOTE	APEX	GOADED

Travels With Charley Vocabular

CONSUMMATE	ORGY	CUR	UBIQUITOUS	KIN
APLOMB	NUISANCE	OGRE	DISPEL	CLOISTERED
ZENITH	WREST	FREE SPACE	PISCINE	DEPLORE
PANDEMONIUM	ANARCHISM	CORPULENCE	ATROPHIED	MISANTHROPY
COURTEOUS	INCISED	MEDIOCRE	PREMISE	TACITURN

Travels With Charley Vocabular

DAWDLE	CONSUMMATE	ELATE	AVID	PERIPATETIC
OBSOLESCENCE	CLOISTERED	PERNICIOUS	INEPT	DEBRIS
CUR	MISANTHROPY	FREE SPACE	INCORRIGIBLE	APEX
VAGUELY	TACITURN	TAWDRY	KIN	OSTENTATION
PRECIOUS	AESTHETIC	SEMANTIC	POSTULATE	VITALITY

Travels With Charley Vocabular

NUISANCE	UBIQUITOUS	ENVOY	CONCISE	DISPEL
PREMISE	FRACAS	CORROBORATE	QUALMS	PARADOX
CONDUCIVE	GALL	FREE SPACE	COERCION	OGRE
VICARIOUS	OBLIQUE	ZENITH	APHIDS	PISCINE
WREST	DOCILE	SUBTLETIES	DEPLORE	VINTAGE

Travels With Charley Vocabular

TAWDRY	POSTULATE	MEDIOCRE	DISPEL	OSTENTATION
CONCISE	ATROPHIED	DOCILE	INEPT	SIEGE
PISCINE	COERCION	FREE SPACE	TACITURN	UBIQUITOUS
CORPULENCE	CONSUMMATE	DEPLORE	PANDEMONIUM	CALLOW
OBSEQUIOUS	PERIPATETIC	APLOMB	GOADED	OBSOLESCENCE

Travels With Charley Vocabular

INALIENABLE	WREST	MISANTHROPY	PERNICIOUS	DEBRIS
NUISANCE	VITALITY	LACONIC	VICARIOUS	CUR
FRACAS	DAWDLE	FREE SPACE	VINTAGE	DECADENT
QUALMS	APHIDS	KIN	SEMANTIC	SUBTLETIES
INCORRIGIBLE	PARADOX	ELATE	ANARCHISM	GALL

Travels With Charley Vocabular

MEDIOCRE	GALL	GOADED	KIN	PRECIOUS
VITALITY	DEBRIS	DEPLORE	LACONIC	PERIPATETIC
CUR	INCISED	FREE SPACE	OGRE	DISPEL
TRAVAIL	PREMISE	APEX	VAGUELY	DOCILE
OSTENTATION	TACITURN	AVID	APLOMB	COURTEOUS

Travels With Charley Vocabular

CLOISTERED	MISANTHROPY	INALIENABLE	ANARCHISM	SIEGE
ENVOY	WREST	INVECTIVES	OBSEQUIOUS	CONDUCIVE
ANTIDOTE	ZENITH	FREE SPACE	ELATE	UBIQUITOUS
TAWDRY	ATROPHIED	DAWDLE	INEPT	SEMANTIC
NUISANCE	INCORRIGIBLE	CORROBORATE	CONCISE	DECADENT

Travels With Charley Vocabular

ATROPHIED	CONDUCIVE	VICARIOUS	VAGUELY	CUR
VITALITY	COERCION	CONCISE	CLOISTERED	KIN
FRACAS	PERNICIOUS	FREE SPACE	OSTENTATION	OBSOLESCENCE
LACONIC	SUBTLETIES	PERIPATETIC	INALIENABLE	APLOMB
PRECIOUS	CALLOW	AESTHETIC	DEPLORE	INVECTIVES

Travels With Charley Vocabular

APHIDS	TACITURN	PISCINE	TAWDRY	COURTEOUS
NUISANCE	GOADED	QUALMS	ANARCHISM	CONSUMMATE
CORROBORATE	TRAVAIL	FREE SPACE	ENVOY	PANDEMONIUM
UBIQUITOUS	DEBRIS	PARADOX	DISPEL	OGRE
SEMANTIC	PREMISE	INCORRIGIBLE	DECADENT	ORGY

Travels With Charley Vocabular

DEPLORE	DEBRIS	INCISED	PISCINE	GOADED
DAWDLE	SIEGE	DOCILE	VINTAGE	COURTEOUS
APHIDS	TAWDRY	FREE SPACE	NUISANCE	POSTULATE
TRAVAIL	GALL	APEX	ANTIDOTE	DISPEL
ENVOY	QUALMS	VITALITY	PREMISE	CORPULENCE

Travels With Charley Vocabular

CONCISE	VICARIOUS	PARADOX	INALIENABLE	PRECIOUS
SUBTLETIES	KIN	LACONIC	CLOISTERED	OGRE
ORGY	ANARCHISM	FREE SPACE	VAGUELY	DECADENT
SEMANTIC	AESTHETIC	PERIPATETIC	COERCION	MEDIOCRE
CONSUMMATE	ATROPHIED	UBIQUITOUS	OBSOLESCENCE	PERNICIOUS

Travels With Charley Vocabular

OSTENTATION	INCORRIGIBLE	AVID	AESTHETIC	PRECIOUS
VITALITY	GALL	SUBTLETIES	LACONIC	INEPT
PISCINE	POSTULATE	FREE SPACE	APHIDS	INVECTIVES
PANDEMONIUM	DOCILE	MEDIOCRE	DISPEL	CONCISE
APEX	OBLIQUE	COURTEOUS	ZENITH	SIEGE

Travels With Charley Vocabular

VAGUELY	CORROBORATE	PARADOX	CALLOW	OGRE
KIN	APLOMB	CONSUMMATE	UBIQUITOUS	CONDUCIVE
CUR	DEPLORE	FREE SPACE	OBSOLESCENCE	DECADENT
COERCION	VINTAGE	PERIPATETIC	MISANTHROPY	CORPULENCE
OBSEQUIOUS	CLOISTERED	VICARIOUS	TACITURN	INALIENABLE

Travels With Charley Vocabular

ZENITH	AESTHETIC	TAWDRY	DECADENT	AVID
APHIDS	QUALMS	WREST	INCISED	APEX
CORROBORATE	GALL	FREE SPACE	TRAVAIL	SUBTLETIES
COURTEOUS	OBSEQUIOUS	CORPULENCE	PANDEMONIUM	DAWDLE
GOADED	OBSOLESCENCE	UBIQUITOUS	SEMANTIC	DISPEL

Travels With Charley Vocabular

CONCISE	POSTULATE	ATROPHIED	ENVOY	CONSUMMATE
OSTENTATION	PARADOX	TACITURN	MISANTHROPY	DEBRIS
PRECIOUS	CUR	FREE SPACE	OGRE	INVECTIVES
VITALITY	VAGUELY	ANARCHISM	PERNICIOUS	CONDUCIVE
COERCION	ANTIDOTE	ORGY	VINTAGE	CALLOW

Travels With Charley Vocabular

PERNICIOUS	OBSEQUIOUS	OGRE	APLOMB	COURTEOUS
ZENITH	CUR	OBLIQUE	SIEGE	CORPULENCE
APEX	CONSUMMATE	FREE SPACE	INCORRIGIBLE	DAWDLE
DEPLORE	FRACAS	CLOISTERED	VICARIOUS	POSTULATE
INVECTIVES	VAGUELY	NUISANCE	PISCINE	TRAVAIL

Travels With Charley Vocabular

VITALITY	INCISED	KIN	ORGY	LACONIC
SEMANTIC	PREMISE	PERIPATETIC	INEPT	CALLOW
MEDIOCRE	GALL	FREE SPACE	PRECIOUS	ANTIDOTE
TAWDRY	OBSOLESCENCE	CONDUCIVE	MISANTHROPY	AESTHETIC
DISPEL	PANDEMONIUM	CONCISE	ENVOY	ATROPHIED

Travels With Charley Vocabular

UBIQUITOUS	AESTHETIC	DISPEL	DEPLORE	PANDEMONIUM
APLOMB	APHIDS	AVID	VICARIOUS	LACONIC
PRECIOUS	TRAVAIL	FREE SPACE	CONDUCIVE	SEMANTIC
DEBRIS	INCISED	PARADOX	TAWDRY	ANTIDOTE
PREMISE	WREST	INCORRIGIBLE	MEDIOCRE	VITALITY

Travels With Charley Vocabular

DOCILE	INVECTIVES	OGRE	CORPULENCE	KIN
CALLOW	PERIPATETIC	CLOISTERED	INEPT	PISCINE
CONCISE	DAWDLE	FREE SPACE	PERNICIOUS	DECADENT
VINTAGE	NUISANCE	ANARCHISM	APEX	OBSEQUIOUS
CORROBORATE	INALIENABLE	SUBTLETIES	CUR	GALL

Travels With Charley Vocabular

ELATE	PISCINE	PERNICIOUS	CORROBORATE	OSTENTATION
ANTIDOTE	CUR	UBIQUITOUS	CONDUCIVE	DOCILE
KIN	WREST	FREE SPACE	VINTAGE	TAWDRY
ORGY	QUALMS	GALL	INEPT	ZENITH
OBSEQUIOUS	INCORRIGIBLE	DAWDLE	DISPEL	AESTHETIC

Travels With Charley Vocabular

SUBTLETIES	POSTULATE	COURTEOUS	PRECIOUS	VITALITY
APEX	OBSOLESCENCE	INCISED	VAGUELY	VICARIOUS
DEBRIS	ENVOY	FREE SPACE	PERIPATETIC	INVECTIVES
APHIDS	AVID	SIEGE	CORPULENCE	PANDEMONIUM
SEMANTIC	CALLOW	APLOMB	COERCION	CONSUMMATE

Travels With Charley Vocabular

AVID	GALL	PISCINE	OSTENTATION	APLOMB
VAGUELY	CONCISE	OGRE	ORGY	LACONIC
QUALMS	VINTAGE	FREE SPACE	ENVOY	MEDIOCRE
CONDUCIVE	AESTHETIC	DISPEL	ANARCHISM	PANDEMONIUM
DECADENT	INEPT	CLOISTERED	CORPULENCE	INVECTIVES

Travels With Charley Vocabular

TACITURN	SEMANTIC	INALIENABLE	ANTIDOTE	ATROPHIED
VITALITY	PERNICIOUS	DOCILE	OBLIQUE	COURTEOUS
OBSOLESCENCE	CONSUMMATE	FREE SPACE	PRECIOUS	DAWDLE
POSTULATE	APEX	CALLOW	CORROBORATE	INCISED
PARADOX	UBIQUITOUS	DEPLORE	ZENITH	FRACAS

Travels With Charley Vocabular

DISPEL	ELATE	CALLOW	APEX	ZENITH
TACITURN	ORGY	FRACAS	GALL	DOCILE
INCISED	CLOISTERED	FREE SPACE	NUISANCE	APLOMB
GOADED	INCORRIGIBLE	ANARCHISM	VINTAGE	INVECTIVES
INALIENABLE	PISCINE	VAGUELY	CUR	PERNICIOUS

Travels With Charley Vocabular

INEPT	COERCION	CORPULENCE	OBLIQUE	WREST
DAWDLE	OSTENTATION	SIEGE	TRAVAIL	PREMISE
AESTHETIC	DEBRIS	FREE SPACE	PARADOX	COURTEOUS
QUALMS	KIN	PANDEMONIUM	OGRE	AVID
CONCISE	UBIQUITOUS	PRECIOUS	PERIPATETIC	MEDIOCRE

Travels With Charley Vocabular

PERIPATETIC	QUALMS	OGRE	SUBTLETIES	PISCINE
OBLIQUE	AVID	ZENITH	DISPEL	TACITURN
OBSEQUIOUS	CUR	FREE SPACE	POSTULATE	LACONIC
SIEGE	VITALITY	DEPLORE	TAWDRY	PARADOX
APEX	INVECTIVES	DOCILE	CLOISTERED	VAGUELY

Travels With Charley Vocabular

INEPT	GALL	OSTENTATION	CALLOW	CORROBORATE
ANTIDOTE	PREMISE	ELATE	ATROPHIED	INCISED
AESTHETIC	KIN	FREE SPACE	PANDEMONIUM	CONSUMMATE
MEDIOCRE	PERNICIOUS	DECADENT	VINTAGE	FRACAS
ENVOY	CORPULENCE	MISANTHROPY	ORGY	SEMANTIC

Travels With Charley Vocabular

TACITURN	DEPLORE	INCISED	DEBRIS	INALIENABLE
DOCILE	UBIQUITOUS	SEMANTIC	QUALMS	ZENITH
APEX	ENVOY	FREE SPACE	DECADENT	CONDUCIVE
PERNICIOUS	DAWDLE	SIEGE	WREST	PARADOX
GALL	APLOMB	CORROBORATE	SUBTLETIES	POSTULATE

Travels With Charley Vocabular

CONCISE	CALLOW	DISPEL	VICARIOUS	NUISANCE
PRECIOUS	CONSUMMATE	VINTAGE	CORPULENCE	OBLIQUE
INVECTIVES	AESTHETIC	FREE SPACE	OBSEQUIOUS	CLOISTERED
COURTEOUS	VITALITY	CUR	TAWDRY	APHIDS
FRACAS	INCORRIGIBLE	INEPT	TRAVAIL	KIN

www.ingramcontent.com/pod-product-compliance
Lightning Source LLC
Chambersburg PA
CBHW081454070526
44586CB00019B/2345